Henry Allen □ Paul Allen □ Yehuda Amichai □ Susan Astor □ Mark H. Baechtel □ John Balaban □ Michelle Boisseau □ Cathy Smith Bowers □ Christopher Buckley □ W. E. Butts □ Grace Cavalieri □ David Chorlton □ Lyn Coffin □ Rhea L. Cohen □ Geraldine Connolly □ Ann Darr □ Michael C. Davis □ Moshe Dor □ Thomas Dorsett □ Denise Duhamel □ Cornelius Eady □ Laura Fargas □ Jane Flanders □ Roland Flint □ Lillian Frankel □ Nan Fry □ Brendan Galvin □ Martin Galvin □ Margaret Gibson □ Albert Goldbarth □ Barbara Goldberg □ Moishe Leib Halpern □ William Heyen □ David Hilton □ Edward Haworth Hoeppner □ William Holland □ Jean Janzen □ Rod Jellema □ Shirley Kaufman □ Deborah Kilgore □ Dorianne Laux □ Barbara F. Lefcowitz □ Merrill Leffler □ Mitchell LesCarbeau □ Susan Ludvigson □ David McAleavey □ Walter McDonald □ Elaine Magarrell □ William Matthews □ José Antonio Mazzotti □ Peter Meinke □ William Meredith □ Leonard Nathan □ Howard Nemerov □ Jean Nordhaus □ Sharon Olds □ Eric Pankey □ Linda Pastan □ Walter Pavlich □ Richard Peabody □ Robert Peters □ Mary Quattlebaum □ John Robert Quinn □ Marilee Richards □ Trish Rucker □ Benjamin Saltman □ Catherine Harnett Shaw □ Enid Shomer □ Layle Silbert □ Myra Sklarew □ R. T. Smith □ Andrew Sofer □ Katherine Soniat □ Stephanie Strickland □ Sue Teigen □ Hilary Tham □ Naomi Thiers □ Lee Upton □ Lloyd Van Brunt □ William Van Wert □ David Walker □ Ronald Wallace □ T. H. S. Wallace □ Nancy G. Westerfield □ Theodore Worozbyt □ Paul Zimmer □ Linda Zisquit □ Henry Allen □ Paul Allen □ Yehuda Amichai □ Susan Astor □ Mark H. Baechtel □ John Balaban □ Michelle Boisseau □ Cathy Smith Bowers □ Christopher Buckley □ W. E. Butts □ Grace Cavalieri □ David Chorlton □ Lyn Coffin □ Rhea L. Cohen □ Geraldine Connolly □ Ann Darr □ Michael C. Davis □ Moshe Dor □ Thomas Dorsett □ Denise Duhamel □ Cornelius Eady □ Laura Fargas □ Jane Flanders □ Roland Flint □ Lillian Frankel □ Nan Fry □ Brendan Galvin □ Martin Galvin □ Margaret Gibson □ Albert Goldbarth □ Barbara Goldberg □ Moishe Leib Halpern □ William Heyen □ David Hilton □ Edward Haworth Hoeppner □ William Holland □ Jean Janzen □ Rod Jellema □ Shirley Kaufman □ Deborah Kilgore □ Dorianne Laux □ Barbara F. Lefcowitz □ Merrill Leffler □ Mitch▪

OPEN DOOR

A POET LORE ANTHOLOGY
1980–1996

OPEN DOOR
A POET LORE ANTHOLOGY
1980–1996

EDITED BY
Philip K. Jason • Barbara Goldberg
Geraldine Connolly • Roland Flint

Writer's Center Editions
Bethesda • Maryland

OPEN DOOR: A *POET LORE* ANTHOLOGY 1980-1996

Cover and book design by Barbara Shaw
Cover adapted from "Open Door," a positive plate offset
by Kevin MacDonald
Production management by Sunil Freeman

Acknowledgments begin on p. 195

ISBN: 0-9654010-0-6
Library of Congress Catalog Card Number: 96-61222

□ □ □

WRITER'S CENTER EDITIONS CO-PUBLICATION SERIES

Ann B. Knox, *Staying Is Nowhere*
(with SCOP Publications)

Michael A. Schaffner, *The Good Opinion of Squirrels*
(with The Word Works)

WRITER'S CENTER EDITIONS
The Writer's Center
4508 Walsh Street
Bethesda, MD 20815

CONTENTS

□ *Contents* □

Contents

□ *Contents* □

FOREWORD

The original impetus for this anthology was to contribute to the twentieth anniversary celebration of the Writer's Center, a well-loved and vital resource in the Washington, DC area and throughout the MidAtlantic region. Since 1987, the Writer's Center has been the publisher of *Poet Lore*.

But the project soon took on a life of its own. After all, *Poet Lore* is the oldest (since 1889) continuously published poetry magazine in the United States. Throughout its history, *Poet Lore* has kept its door open, providing a home to the well known, the less well known, and the unknown. The Writer's Center also stands by that policy.

What you will find in *Open Door* is a poet's eye view of the late twentieth century. It is the news that never grows old. The voices are as rich and various as our preoccupations. Some speak from the reaches of the past—we meet St. John of the Cross, John Keats, Mary Cassatt, and the wife of God; others beguile us with a funky vernacular, as in "I ought not to story so, I guess" ("Youngblood Tells Beekman and Jimmy Jr. About Crow," by Paul Allen). The images range from starkly lyrical: "A good cold morning / has the startled eye of a bird" ("Trout Run," by Rod Jellema), to dense and unsparing: "Again, as if it were another life / Reviewed, the heaped up mass of rusty cars" ("Waste," by Howard Nemerov), and "I knifed / my white Caddy / into the city / where I got fingered / as alternate juror / in an Hispanic murder case" ("Stiletto," by William Heyen). One poem ("Responsibility" by Moshe Dor) suggests, "You know, / perhaps we misread our time, this place. Perhaps / we were meant to breathe in a different rhythm, to use / different words."

We think not. For isn't uncertainty also a pervasive obsession of our era?

In celebrating the Writer's Center's twenty years, we celebrate the contributions of many individuals and supportive organizations. We celebrate talent and friendship, learning and giving, exploration and growth.

Thanks are due to the nominating board for this anthology: David Bristol, Sarah Cotterill, Ann Darr, Moshe Dor, Rod Jellema, Beth Joselow, Merrill Leffler, Chris Llewellyn, Jean Nordhaus, Linda Pastan, Richard Peabody, Frederick Pollack, Henry Taylor, Hilary Tham, and Reed Whittemore. We note with gratitude past managing editors—Kate Curry, Ed Taylor, Susan Davis, and Margaret Buckley—for getting out the issues in which these poems first appeared. We remember the late Kevin Madden for his contribution of many years and also our long-time coworker, Barbara Lefcowitz. And we applaud Sunil Freeman, managing editor of *Poet Lore* since 1988, for his invaluable help on this project.

Finally, we thank our publishers, Jane Fox and Allan Lefcowitz, who are respectively Executive Director and Artistic Director of the Writer's Center. We offer *Open Door* to you for your pleasure, and to honor the Writer's Center, twenty years old, still young at heart.

Barbara Goldberg and Philip K. Jason
Project Directors

JAPANESE AMBASSADOR

Late each night
the Japanese ambassador
walks his dachshund
from streetlight to streetlight.
A bodyguard, square head, silk suit,
trails in shadow.
The ambassador dreams
of being a cowboy in a rain
of frogs and bicycles.
The bodyguard imagines
a huge, sunny railroad station
waiting room, its lacquered gold
information booth
like a legendary toy birdcage.
The dog practices holding its breath.

Youngblood Tells Beekman and Jimmy Jr. About Crow

I'll tell you what I know, but it's no use,
you'll have to learn another way to make
it true for you. Today you're going to kill
crow. (Watch yourself; I have to get there.)
I'll stay home and try to make the creek
go east a hundred yards or so and back
up just beyond those pin oaks there.
Besides, I got no use for shooting crows,
but that's no reason you two boys should stay.

The sun will do me good. Miss Evelyn likes
me home. Now when you get there (move) stand
for a little while away from your guns, say
over by Old Doc Allison's truck. You watch,
the men will end up there, so that puts you
in with them so to speak, but not too eager.
When they break up to get themselves a stand,
you two go together. This ain't like killing
dove where you want to get a stand that lets
you have a larger field of vision—alone
and still, you can have a dove. He'll come for you,
but crow—you ought to be in shadow or down
for crow, or under something like a pine—
something man put there so the crow's accustomed.
And you will have to call them in to you.

See what you got to do is hurt one soon
as possible, a young one full of fear
and hurt, that still has strength with number 6
in his gut, one who'll fall but doesn't know
enough to die and flops and carries on.
His flapping and loud dying helps you out.
The old ones (Watch yourself), it seems the fall
kind of hurts them special; they bleed in the throat
and don't say anything and give up quick.

I've known it to happen. They just don't seem to care.
But aim true, now. I'm not saying miss.
You will, though. One you'll only hurt, and that's
your one. (Take this.) Tie him to a piece
of board out a ways; too close to you
and he'll be too still, too far and he'll feel alone
and won't do much. Nineteen, twenty feet
and he'll know you're there and try to get away.

That one will bring a hundred in to you
and you'll get your fill of shooting, all you want.
Crows can't stand the suffering of their own—
like folks at a wreck. They ain't coming to help;
they're not like doves. You shoot a dove, you go out
and get him. Pull his head off quick, right there,
to settle him down and drain the meat for eating,
and bring him back with you, hide him like.
But let a shot crow, dead or hurt, just lay.

(I got what I need here. Hop in. I'll take
you far as the gate. Blow that cup out and pour
me one from this. I've got work to do.)
Crows are close to us if evolution
is not made up. That's why you need to hunt
them in the spirit of fun. What about
"he had to eat crow," when they mean embarrassed
and having to take back something he spoke out.
A bunch of crows is a "murder." Did you know that?
Now there's a human word if ever was.
Of course don't call them that around the men;
they'll think you're like that woman here last spring
on her study. Or how about the famous crow
in ancient days that sat on a picture of Jesus
and kept on saying "Nevermind"? (What's that?)
I don't know if crows can really talk
but they know what to say if they're a mind.
Don't matter.

Some fancy britches may come out
from town that brings a silly record player
calling crow. Crap. More than most
animals, crows just can't decide; they're not
like coon or possum that have gone ahead and claimed
garbage cans and attics in old homes
and look so dead on Old Towne Road.
But crow do want us so, just can't adjust.
So they like those records of men acting like crows.
If the others let him have the record player,
you just come on back. Might's well walk down
to the pond and shoot cow pies all day or help
me, I could use a hand. (Hold this.)

It won't matter whether you kill or not.
You'll probably be the youngest, so the main
thing is to keep your barrel hot; the men,
they'll gather back at Doc Allison's truck.

They'll just form a natural circle and they'll spit.
They'll sort of put the whole day in the middle
and look at it awhile. If you killed enough
they'll say it. They always put the youngest boys
like you, who's hardly started hair there yet,
inside the day and rib him. That's good. Be glad.
(Let me have one more to start my day.)
They'll let you know you did o.k. by them.
Like one will say, "Young Beekman's got the eye."
And they'll say, "Yep." And "Yep." And "Jimmy Junior's
rare on a 20." Even if you don't
kill, and you will, so long's you did all right
they'll say something. They'll say you started a legend
for the county, setting the whole damn sky on fire.
Just keep your barrel hot. But only on crow.

But what the men can't stand is indecision—
waffling at the kill, farting around.
Like ducking when a braver crow dives down

to see the wounded crow from how you see it.
Or worse, being squat down and pointing
at one coming out of the sun and failing to shoot
cause another's heading toward the sun,
you swing around to him but a big one's coming
straight at you and one behind, and then
you've lost your balance and plump down on your ass
and all them crows go back to where they came
and you've had your daddy's gun in all directions
and nothing's dead except the sky and your story.
They'll be quiet on you then at the truck.

(O.K. Here. Now I can't turn her off.
She might sit and I would lose a day.
You got time. I'll just finish this off.)
You'll do all right. I can't tell you nothing.
I've said more than I thought to anyway.
I got work to do, and you got crow.
I've told you more than I ever said to that gal
from Vanderbilt, and she had a government grant
to ask about place names in Alabama.
And she was from Ohio, anyway.
Selma. Or-ville. Minter. Car-low-ville—
you should have heard the way she read that list.
She ought to make a record, might bring in crow.
I give her names. Made them up right there,
but she didn't know it; shows you what she knew:
Poot Hollar. Stump Broke. Slap-Your-Pappy.
Miss Evelyn didn't speak to me for a week,
but I give her the money anyway for the house.
Place names! And her with no true place to be.
That kind of thing ought to be done by a woman
whose children are moved off and she's lived there.
I ought not story so, I guess.
        Get gone.
Pull the handle hard. You boys do good,
then come on home and tell me how you did.

□ *Yehuda Amichai* □

(translated by Chana Bloch)

FROM SONGS OF ZION THE BEAUTIFUL

On the last words of Trumpeldor,
It is good to die for our country, they built
the new homeland, like hornets in crazy nests.
And even if those were not his exact words,
or he never said them, or if he did and they drifted away,
they are still there, vaulted like a cave. The cement
has gotten harder than stone. This is my homeland
where I can dream without stumbling,
do bad deeds without being lost,
leave my wife without feeling lonely,
cry without shame, lie and betray
without going to hell for it.

This is the land we covered with field and forest
but we had no time to cover our faces
so they are naked in the grimace of sorrow and the ugliness of joy.

This is the land whose dead lie in the ground
instead of coal and iron and gold:
they are fuel for the coming of messiahs.

□ *Yehuda Amichai* □

(translated by Chana Bloch)

14

Because of the will of the night, I left the land
of the setting sun.
I came too late for the cedars, there weren't any left.
I also came too late for A. D. Gordon, and most of the swamps
were already drained when I was a child.

But my held-back weeping
hardened the foundations. And my feet, moving
in desperate joy, did what ploughs do,
and pavers of roads.
And when I became a man, the voice
of Rachel-weeping-for-her-children broke too.

My thoughts come back to me toward evening
like those who harvested in the days of Degania, in dust and joy.
On top of the hay-wagon.

Now I live in a city of hills where it gets dark
before it does at the seashore.
And I live in a house that gets dark before it does outside.
But in my heart, where I really live,
it's always dark.
Perhaps one day there will finally be light
as in the far North.

THE WIFE OF GOD

Since woman's work is never done
She's busy night and night until the sun
Divides her hours into days.
He does not praise her, for He knows
This is the life she wants, and chose
Though He suspects she did not quite suppose
Eternity was *endless*.
For eons, she airs out the sky,
Plumps up the clouds and wonders why
She has no friends.
Meanwhile, He's omnipresent elsewhere
Inspecting planets, lustering the hair of angels.
She fills the oceans, spreads the spring,
Distributes wildlife, everything He is
Too wise to be concerned with.
Like every good wife everywhere,
She makes notations, answers prayers,
Keeps track of constellations.
Each century, she serves him wine
With love (albeit non-divine)
And asks politely if the world will end;
How many miracles they can afford to spend.
He's gruff; His booming answers make her cry.
She wonders when He plans to die.

NEIGHBORS

Eight years we have been close and distant in this way
You, the sweet gum and the pebbled flower beds.
Me, the stub of chestnut and the homebuilt boat.
As far as I can remember, we have never spoken.

Your name is ambiguous
Like the name of #43 when I was growing up.
"The Dancers" I would overhear
And I was never sure if it was their last name
Or their profession, or just a reference
To the Christmas reindeer on their roof.

Our garbage is picked up on the same days.
Our lights go out during the same storms.
And now, late afternoon, the only ones outdoors,
October holds us both.

A tall tree casts a shadow on the pavement.
For a longer and longer moment
The shadow considers us like a thumb.

We are being painted into the same picture:
The rust of my hair,
The brown of your corduroy.
The sun spreads over us.
I feel you pause when I do.
We cannot look up for the brightness.
Even if we were friends,
We could not speak.

WINDOW, NORTH CHARLES STREET

The failing light that falls upon the walks tonight
Is golden as the light that might be falling now
On the Acropolis.
This isn't Greece—it's Baltimore
Where Fell's Point is at least as dear
As any scruffy, white-washed alleyway
Whose name's a mumble in an alphabet you cannot read.
The air is ripe with ancientness along the harbor pier;
Your hand on mine is as mysterious
As ruins, the sound of mandolins in bars, ouzo in small glasses.
And in the yards of St. Charles Village
The crickets are like creaking doors
That drift in winds that carry voices of
Returning fishermen.

In this one narrow bed we have been travelers;
Have called the light that slumbers from the moon
Rare, delicious, strange as any glancing
From the grottos of Greek seas.
I've moved my lips along your throat
And found an island in the hollow at its base—
Aegean, blue; its only town is Baltimore:
The gentle, mundane capital of dying cars
That cruises tonight with a startled, foreign grace;
That, from your bedroom window, could be
Almost anyplace.

SNOWBOUND

Tragedies of clouds still stumble over us
stalled in cars and tractor trailers
along the highway blocked at a mountain pass,
but now a track team from a chartered bus
has shoved a van past a jack-knifed trailer
and so, after long hours, a lane is cleared
for all the bickering parents and bratty kids
for truckers zonked on speed and nattering on CBs
for the long-hauler with straggly hair and no front teeth
who struck out in the snow to straighten things out
and who stomped back angry, for the snoozing salesmen
for the old folks too shy to pee by the road
for the teenagers yelling in hormonal fits
for the wailing babies, for the diabetic
shooting his thigh behind a fogged windshield
for the lovers feeling lucky at being trapped together
and just wishing it were night
for all of us now inching forward in a glittering line
resuming our lives under a sweep of clearing sky.

□ *John Balaban* □

FOR MY SISTER IN WARMINSTER GENERAL HOSPITAL

The two birds augured something strange.
First, I saved the blackpoll warbler
that piped twice as the cat pounced
and raked its claws about the slapping wings.
No blood, but the bird couldn't fly.
It pecked the cup of my warm hands
and slept that night in a bamboo creel.
Freed the next morning, it peeped
and bounded to a hemlock
where it cocked its head at me
and then flew off to Argentina.

Next, the junco sitting by the door.
I scooped it up, making another nest
of hands as I carried it inside.
When I let it loose later in the day
it bobbed away in the little arcs
that juncos make from bush to bush.
Two birds in the same day. Just exhausted.

I've heard of whole migrations blown off course,
looking for the Orkneys, lost in the Atlantic,
plummeting like hail onto a passing ship
where they flopped, faltered, and died.
All about, birds falling into the swells.
So these auguries were for you, my sister,
asthmatic, gasping to flex your lungs
for ten days, or so I learned tonight.

When I was small and could not breathe
you read me comics: Little Lulu and Scrooge McDuck
were our favorites. You read or made them up

while your skinny brother sat like a board in bed
and wheezed and panic widened in his eyes.

But I rested and flew off.
Thirty years later, you force your lungs for air.
Consider: whole flocks lost and blown into the sea.
Consider the sailors looking from that deck,
watching the waves engulf the keening birds.
It makes no sense; it only happens.

You be the bird that fell down exhausted,
that rested and took off, a bit later in the day.

TIMBRE

Half-naked on the table, I hardly think
of what my doctor listens for, stepping
the cool bell of the stethoscope

across my belly. The day's last patient,
I lie quiet in her quiet examining room
as the buildings around us recover

their lulled latitudes—the bank emptied
of tellers, telephones easing off
in the offices like bland headaches.

Only later do I recognize this
as the hushed moment before entrances.
In the orchestra pit, horns and bows

lifted in readiness. The slightest
agitation of the curtains
as if even the drapery anticipated

the spangled garb: dark and brilliant,
someone throws sequins onto a swift stream.
I'm half-asleep when my doctor hands me

the earpieces, and there you are,
fetal heart, minute percussionist, bareback rider
hurrying toward us in your own good time.

THUNDER

My husband calls
from his month-long trip to California
still nursing the anger
he left me holding like a small child
in the dwindling window of the airport

and hears from my side of the continent
the crack of thunder
and yes, yes
that is what he misses most
about South Carolina

not the dust rising
in red puffs above the corn,
not the lakes of carp and catfish
turning deep
in their tentative dreams of flight

but the way
when the land is long given up for dead
and farmers have disinherited the sky
for good this time
it breaks sudden and big as forgiveness.

They don't have that here, he says
as if he were speaking
of grits or Dixie Beer
or a woman
who would stand in a storm
holding the receiver to the sky.

CONVERSATION WITH MY HYPHEN AFTER THE DIVORCE

Because neither name
made commotion enough to matter,
I jambed you there
like a doorstop
between the bed and bath
of love's vacation house
and kept them both.

Stay! Stay! I cried
pointing my finger,
and like a good dog
you whimpered once
and lay down.

Now, you are an orphan
left on my backporch step.
You have lost your sweetness.
You have lost your teeth.

You poke about these empty rooms
like my grandmother's old nose.
Stake without a garden.
Length of firewood that will not burn.

You little amputee,
mutation with no thumb
trailing my name like a proffered hand
no one wants to shake.

When the moon is full
you are my broomstick.
We make our rounds,

an item as they say,
cackling through the night
at my own bad joke.

When dawn brings us home
I lay you down beside me
in the dark.

PRIMA FACIE

I've always liked the old story of Bertrand Russell
giving a public lecture on astronomy, and a woman
standing up afterwards to say it was all rubbish,
that the earth was really flat and supported
on the back of a giant tortoise! And when Russell
asked just what the turtle was standing on,
the woman was ready and replied, "Why, it's turtles
all the way down."
　　　　　　Doesn't it add up this flawlessly
while we take our short swim off these rocks—
stunned in the immediate and febrile good will
of the light as it replays every summer
traveling home from the shore, green sea
still sparkling in our veins, horizon's blue frame
holding, crepuscular, one star only burning
there and inside of us in continuous disputation
of the dark...
　　　　　　And again this evening, I'm watching
a feckless delegation of clouds depart for home,
or perhaps the rain-emptied coast of Dieppe, I'm brooding
on immortality where once white sandwich wrappers
lifted above the chalk-dull cliffs and seagulls argued
low along a flinty sea blown back along the quai
as if there were another element to the light that we,
stalled there and as simple as those wind-thinned trees,
were letting slip away...
　　　　　　A carnival had cleared off
over night and papers scuttled on the long green field,
a red and yellow poster waving from a bench, were little
to say time and space had been put to use there and then,
and in that way—unremarkable now and shuffling off
with the salt shifting of the air.
　　　　　　A wafer of sun
cut across the clouds' grey scroll, the black edges

of night bleeding in until bright specks floated up
on the blank plate of space with all our unsupported
paradigms for science and for art—the dark ocean
spattered with refracted light like the grainy surface
of the soul—both perhaps expanding, still being etched
with the lost music of the spheres—while we were only
at sea again in our hearts, pointing out first hand the old
shapes and overlappings, the sure and selfsame stars.

Martin's Nursing Home

Black ladies in pink dresses walk and wheel
the dying into the solarium. A woman,
like someone recalling an adolescent love,
cannot name what she had for dinner,
but insists it was very good. A man points
at a bookcase, and claims he read every book
before he came here, then says, "But that's not
the whole story of my life." There's something
sinister about the way the dusty windows refuse
to allow winter light to enter the room.
This is a place where the old surrender the day
to a bite of forbidden candy, or a long,
heavenly pull from what may be the last cigarette.
Television announces the news above
their bowed heads, and the cracked tile floor.
Afternoons, they wait in the cold, grave lobby
for the visitor that never comes, then reminisce
over the children who could have treated them well.
Once a month, there are two glasses of wine
in the basement, and the required dance.

LES JARDINS

See the cold birds
By the red brick boathouse near the water
Their cold beauty
Disguised like a motive,
Small birds in the door in the wall,
Where the answer lay.

Someone is whistling. It is dark.
It is the man overpaying the bill
Then apologizing to the barmaid.
I mistook the light for sun and closed the door.

Who can say his gesture is from love?
And that it is to wrap his hands in silk
And to stroke his arms that he does such things?

Matters are not what they seem to be
Or as we wish they were.
Take the barmaid,
The blonde keeps sacrificing herself
Acting dumber and dumber and getting
Farther and farther from what she is feeling

Lighter and lighter, her head is surrounded
By a halo of light, but now, fully mechanized
Her actions and feelings not one,
The voice gets higher and higher. Her anger lowers,
Cutting the girl in two.

Her head spins about from down the street. She
Complains that the rest of her body would
Wake her up to reject her. "I'm going to grow
And paint my fingernails" she calls back to herself.

She decides to be happy
She decides to be angry
She plans to move to the red brick boathouse
By the water
To feed the cold birds.

Her customer intends to cancel
His subscription to *The New Republic*
In order to express his needs and his rage.

They give each other a Christmas present
Then throw it out with the tissue paper
If they had enough they wouldn't worry
About what was lost
She thinks her mind is trying to kill her body
He wants to pay her for a kiss
"My feelings are my lips" she says.

Years later I passed a pile of old clothes
And knew they'd come that way.
The blanket
Holding all that was warm from them,

Placing a book on the ground, I hid
To see who would pick it up to read,
They came into sight
He said it was entitled: THE RICH OUTPOURINGS
OF A FERTILE MIND
She said it was entitled: THE RICH IMAGININGS
OF A GREAT MIND.

If I could only say what I felt for them
I'd say nothing.
The blonde barmaid said "I would hate anyone
To feel the way about me that I feel about

Everyone else."
Her customer jumped into the air and clicked
His heels.

Lately the barmaid and her customer stay
In a penthouse near the water.
The trick is to get to the window from
The top floor and crawl down
The outside wall from the roof and then
Invite everyone over for Thanksgiving dinner.

The nurse told her that if in making love
The perspiration from his forehead went into
Her nose and up to her brain, the baby would be
Born intelligent. Afterwards she asked
The nurse why her body ached. The nurse said
"I don't know" and moved her off the bed
For the next patient.

Sometimes I will catch just a glimpse of
Them, the front of his sweater or a part of her skirt;
The way her skirt catches on her leg
And it will make me love them, but just for a brief
Second and just for that time

Cheer up. Whatever they feel now, they'll feel
Something else later.
"Do you want some orange juice?" he said and
She said "No thank you."
At the table he said "I didn't know she
Wanted some orange juice." I said "I
Didn't either." He said to her "I'm sorry
I didn't hear you say you wanted some orange juice."

I thought I saw myself across the room
And excused myself but it was only

The barmaid wearing a white gown
Her hood was empty. She sat on the chair,
Her hood fell off. She fell on the floor,

She is dead, I thought. I rushed
Back to tell them, to ask what
Part of myself she represented, such a
Versatile instrument, such a curious set of
Circumstances, not my feelings or my defenses

But something in between. The customer and the barmaid
Claimed that nothing I did happened,
As a guest, they put me to sleep in the mud,
My thumb pulled outside a hole in the board for air,
It grows crooked to this day.

One day I woke and said I smelled something awful on me
Like mud,
They said, No, We held you all night in our arms with
Love by the red brick boathouse near the water.

ST. JOHN OF THE CROSS IN THE CARMELITE PRIORY, TOLEDO, 1578

A horse is waiting to enter the country of silence.
Water returns to the stars there, space
is the substance of dreams. I hear a song

outside my prison, it is dying of love,
O, what shall I do? Alahé,
just die, alahé. What a cold night.
Wind pulls fingers through my hair,

and breath of the stars makes tunnels
in my flesh. Small creatures

eat and love there. They must see
the glow at the end
that opens into me, where filth
becomes the flame of spirit.

A pen, dear jailer,
this must be written while I smile,
for tomorrow they will whip

flies off my shoulders. I shall thank them
standing, before they roll me
back into this stone

where my own waste pushes
me into the corner
and beyond. How I love you, thorn

that searches for the rose within me.
I am bent
but a soul has no shape.

The light of my body is riding
to her bed. My shoulders bow

in front of my heart. Out of this rugged land,
a river guides the horse.

STONE WINE

"And we'll all drink stone wine
when Johnny comes marching home..."

He weaves his way home—one large, weather-reddened
Hand trailing an empty bottle. When he gets to
The place where the trees close in on him,
He is a brigadier again. Thus,
The empty bottle becomes a cane and
He is on assignment in Africa
Or India—batting away the swarming
Arms of the dusky little buggers who
Try to embarrass and impede him ... By the time
He has climbed the front steps and entered
The glassed-in front porch, he no longer holds
His bottle by the neck: he grasps the base
Firmly in his left hand and opens the inner
Door, liking the feel of the brass doorknob in
One hand, the glass bottle in the other—the round
Balance of those two cold, smooth things. He walks
With not at all comic stealth across
The carpeted hallway and opens the door
Under the stairs, the door to what she
Always insists on calling "the guest
Bathroom." He doesn't fumble for the light
As usual, but points his bottleglass rifle
Where he knows the toilet to be cowering
Like a yellow-bellied gook. "Halt!" he cries. "Halt!
Who goes there? Who's doing what in my bathroom?"
Now he nods at the dark, shadowy sea below
Him, the unblooded hordes who speak to him
With the round dark mouths of guns: first in silence,
Then in a roar, then in the darkness which is
Both, and before... He tosses the bottle
In the wastebasket, his memory a high flare

In whose light the hand-grenade explodes, but
Turns out to be nothing more patriotic
Than a firecracker at a children's party...
He turns and climbs the stairs, not remembering past drills,
Past exercises where he was made to climb—
Remembering nothing, he does as he's been
Taught—because the doing must be all, must be
Automatic. Otherwise...Otherwise, you have
...The woman... She will be lying in bed,
A clock and a glass at her elbow, a book
Open in her hands. She will be on the edge
Of a circle of soft light, in a nightdress
That shows everything, again. She will say she has been
Waiting. He will nod... Despite himself, he will answer
And tell her: "Those who wait are empty."

□ Rhea L. Cohen □

MARY CASSATT, PUPIL OF EDGAR DEGAS

I burned
his letters. Lovers?
With that common little man?

To me he'd say,
Stay with what you know
(and mean: Leave *my* themes alone).
To others he brayed, No woman
can draw that well.
That cock-fool crowed, I could
have wed her, but I
could not have made love to her.

Well we loved light.
Unjuried
the work our prize.
                    What then
caused it? Think of Renoir…
all of us…squinting into color
as if through seared eyes
and of Edgar's fingers
those last dark days, caressing
fresh clay—elemental
    the way the clay
quickened to limbs
sinuous hip and shoulder
    the clay in his hands
undulant a lifting
a lifting up of her chin
    the way the clay
in his hands

acquiesced.
    Yes.

But was it the pigments
was it that radiation cure
Or: Had we drawn too close?

Renoir and Monet lost
most of their sight. Pissarro
and he
and then I
in total blindness died.

CLIMBING UP TO THE ATTIC

for Lish Mahler

Open it, she says.
It is shut tight. I trace
its block shape like the letter of some

new alphabet. I open my hand
and a small light appears.
Open it, she says.

If I open it
all the cold wind, ice and night
the cobwebs will fly in.

And, if you don't open it, she asks.
I will be safe
my fingers counted, my hair snug on my head.

The watchers will no longer keep watch.
The key, I add, will not fit.
The hinges could have rusted by now,

or twisted into licorice.
If I open it, I say, and step in
floorboards might give way

the mandolins will have broken strings.
I am pleading now. There is a stinking lake
a long stair with broken dolls at the top.

Behind them, a red-faced clown waits.
All of the doves will be gone.
You can open it, she says.

What Do You Want from the Country?

My heart is in my mouth
as I grab the paddle with
both hands and swing the canoe
prow into the sluiceway
between the rocks. Now
there is no turning back.

There never was.
I only thought
there was.

I have brought
my choicest small things
to surround me here in my tower
above the square, the small ceramic
sheep-vase, with the ceramic
wooly head (clay pushed through
a garlic press), the quilted
piece-work pillow picture of
our farm, complete with
the Blue Ridge in the background
(those Articles set forth in
Schedule B, attached hereto,
What do you want from
the Country?)
        I want the goddamned
mountain! and I want it entire!
and I want it now! and I want
my flock of birds with the indigo
bunting and the song of the lark
and I want them whenever I care
to listen, and I want the banks
of bluebells by the river

and the river running as far
as I can see and the canoe
under me and me able to take
the riffles (not the white water,
I wasn't good at white water)
but the riffles around the great
rocks, "All right! Here we
go!" and I could guide us through,
I who was raised in dry country,
corn country, could finally meet
the water challenge and feel
the exhilaration of a small sweet
success without which we live
our lives in colors of gray,
without the sun, without, without.
We live in a lack, the nebulous
missing, we live in the shallows of
sand, the dull...is it then,

that I have chosen the pain on
purpose? As better than the nothing,
the void? Have I fallen into
one of the scientist's pockets,
those who have a name for
the pain-hunters? Masochism squared?

What do I want from the country?

I want my copperhead from under the porch!
I want the lotus blooming in the mornings,
they close in the afternoon. They are too
fragile to carry into town as we once
planned to make our fortune selling lotus
blossoms to the florists, that was when
we decided to make our fortune selling
lotus *root* to the food houses, or to
the freaky houses, or to anyone who wanted

love to spring swiftly from some root to
their root, some sweet enhancement of sex
(which we, clever minds that we had,
should have seen was a false claim, else
why did we wander off in separate directions
every time the company left, the friends
departed). *So long! Wonderful weekend,*
marvelous steaks, gorgeous boat trip,
heavenly wildflowers, great outdoor
dancing, loved your fire....

I want the fire, the fireplace I carried
the stones for, chose the lintel for
the mantel, the hearthstones and
carried them myself from the quarry
near Potomac to the mountainside
where the old stonemason sweated
and cursed me under his breath when
I insisted that the mantel stones
be placed with the raw side out
because I didn't want a neat and
tidy edge to the mantel, and I didn't
really understand until much later
what I must have done to his soul,
his soul of a stonemason, to tidy
the work, to respect the line of

the stone, to still put his name
on this work, this high rising fire-
place of granite from the Blue Ridge
via the tumbled house of old Billy
Mitchell who was fired from
the Army in disgrace because he said
back in 192? that some Sunday
morning the Japanese would fly
over Pearl Harbor and...
they taught him not to tell lies,

expelled him from the ranks, took
away his medals. A little late
they reinstated him in a museum.
His son, our Blue Ridge neighbor,
told how hard it is to be
a great man's son. Papa,
you weren't a great man, but you
were a loving man. Why did I help
keep you from the woman you loved?
Was I still trying to keep you for
myself?

What do I want from the country?
The ghost of my Papa, the farmer,
who walked those meadows with me,
who taught me how to camp from
Iowa to California, who finally
gave me his blessing to learn
to fly.

What do I want from the country?

I want the well I dowsed
with its cold pure water, water
which cannot put out the fire
I also dowsed.

HRASNO

"Part of the loaf was gone, and what remained, still grasped
in his right hand, attracted flocks of pigeons that settled
near the body, seemingly oblivious to volleys of tank fire that
had everyone within blocks running for cover."
                                          — *New York Times*, 10/8/92

Each morning I slide the withered legs
into the same old gray trousers
and don the same gray jacket.
I hoist one stale loaf of bread
in the crook of my arm and leave
to feed the souls of the dead.

Between the battered homes
snipers' bullets chirp
like the last cries of sparrows
caught in a trap.
My heart is caged, too,
trembling in a thicket.

They will come from the sky
on wings like snow,
descending without sound onto the slates
paving the ruined square.
My mother, in an iridescent dress
with her eye fixed and unblinking;

my father, dark winged and white breasted,
his head erect and his step firm. My sister,
preening, dead these long years by her own hand.
The bread crumbles in my fist. To dust.
Dust. Each day passes as if
my ear were pressed to an hourglass—

Each grain hissing
as it is pinched, passing
into darkness. The wings clamor
and rise from the walkway as the meal is spread.
A red feather rises in my throat
as the snipers close. They will be fed.

□ *Moshe Dor* □

(translated by Catherine Harnett Shaw)

BASIC VOCABULARY

The Inuit, at home in the eternal ice, have thirty
words for snow to tell its shape, its hues,
the taste of it, its sounds.

I'm thinking now, in the hushed glow of the evening lamp,
still gasping, sweat gleaming
on my upper lip, the shadows blue

under your eyes, how
the old miner I've become refuses
to give up, stripping layer

after layer of this clumsy language off, to excavate
that single word and then exhale it, warm
into the dark, that place between your breasts.

☐ *Moshe Dor* ☐

(translated by Erella Hadar, Myra Sklarew, and the author)

RESPONSIBILITY

At my feet a female dog lies as if in an old English
painting. Through my window, for the first time
in many days, transparent air flows in. You know,
perhaps we misread our time, this place. Perhaps
we were meant to breathe in a different rhythm, to use
different words. Now the wind passes without
any resistance in a sky emptied of planes and no one
shouts to us "Halt!" And no one wonders
how it is possible to pass in this way, without even one
shout of warning or the rattle of a rifle lock or the thud
of soldiers' boots, heavy with responsibility,
as they approach the barricades.

THE ARSONIST

Boxes and files in the basement
await us. Let us make love.
Combustibles changed by a match
shall sing at the wedding—
Alarms shall announce our red guests;
we'll make bureaucrats dance for life.

We'll make the staff eat ceiling cake
served on heated floors; devils
shine like seraphim around
their jealous Lord! In my office, my angel,
you will submit to the glow on my face
while squealing pigs roast in their stalls.

LITERARY BARBIE

When Barbie reads Kafka's *The Metamorphosis,*
her whole body aches. She relates
to Gregor Samsa, the salesman-turned-bug,
who tries to explain the transformation
to his family, but who can only
produce tiny insect-squeaks. So many times
that kind of thing has happened to her.
Barbie's ouches gone unacknowledged, silent giggles
indicating appreciated tickles, lost shrill cries for help.
From the other room, she overhears a human telling her friend
that women make Barbie-feet just before orgasm,
pointing their bare toes to the edge
of the bed, even though they aren't wearing high heels.
Barbie has a thought, unsure whether it is
memory or pure imagination:
                                    It's her, but not her,
under the stars, in field of wet grass. She looks
like someone she doesn't know—a chubby girl
with problem skin and thick glasses. There is a hand,
her own or someone else's, between her legs
and she feels the beginnings of something
she's never felt before. In her terror of pleasure,
she whispers no to it all. And wakes up, immobile,
plastic, looking entirely like somebody else.

MISS JOHNSON DANCES FOR THE FIRST TIME

When Ophelia met the water
It was a gentle tumble of a dance
A mixed marriage of a dance.
The swans were confused.
She was a contradiction in terms.
She was, simply put, a beautiful death.

Not so with Miss Johnson
A wheat field of a girl
Who held her breath
As she cast herself on the dance floor
In a metallic blue dress

At the Grange Hall on Saturday Night,
Holding on to a skinny mechanic

Who knew two steps
That could be shown in public.

It was like being pushed off the raft by her Father:
The awful moment when the body believes in nothing.
How ridiculous her body looked

How her brothers loved to remind her:
A wharf rat.
A drowned cow.

When Amelia Earhart met the water,
Assuming, of course, that she met the water,
Did the sea mistake her for a bird
Or a flying fish?

In the awkward moment she belonged neither to sea
      nor air
Did she move like Miss Johnson moves now,

Bobbing
Like a buoy at high tide,
Gulping mouthfuls of air
As her legs learn the beat and push,
And her blue dress catches the mechanic's pant leg
Like an undertow?

Psyche

Whatever it is, it goes out of reach.
Might as well turn into butterflies,
as she did. Veneration of the empty house
is a lonesome mania—flowers for Valentino
year after year, full-blown roses
shriveling above a body the giver never touched.

JOHN KEATS, APOTHECARY

He did not die after all in Rome, the winter
of '21, but gradually gained back
what he had almost lost to the sloe-eyed muse
slithering off into a brackeny dell.

In May Mother and I arrived, taking rooms
near the Piazza di Spagna. Birds sang
all night. The trees sighed with flowers.
"Fanny," he cried, "*you* are my Indian maid!"
And the Moon turned her face, like a pressed gardenia, away.

We came home together in August. He would have stayed
in the sun's demesne, the shouts of—he said—angels
surging through his portals like summer vines,
but Mother and I missed our green, shady clime.

We were married here in Hempstead in late September.
With time he established a modest practice, including
a little surgery, though he never stops hating
their screams. (We have heard, lately, ways have been found
to let flesh dream, while the knife works deftly on.)

This pleasant life has made me a bit stout.
I can hardly remember that harem-scarem girl
who teased him out of his bookish ways. Tom,
our eldest, attends Cambridge. Georgina delights
in music and Madeline claims she is writing a novel.

Mother died a year ago in her sleep.
I keep the shop, tend garden, while he putters
around the laboratory, still seeking
a cure for consumption, suspects it may be contagious.

Once in a while a stranger like you stops by
to talk of the past, taking a turn about

as if we kept our simples in Grecian urns,
bringing up Truth and Beauty, but he just laughs,
"In my youth I wrote poetry—as almost everyone does.
Would you care to try my new elixir for gout?"

PIGEON IN THE NIGHT

Feels a little black hole in his chest
And knows it to be his heart,
Dense with the gravid night,
A black invisible diamond weighing in
With the accumulation of its losses,
The cruel impacted build-up, the loss
Especially this morning, drawing all the others into it,
Of his own right hand, his heart itself,
For a while, his son gone forever.
He can't quite hang on to pigeon when
The night bores in like this.

□ *Lillian Frankel* □

TEN YEARS AFTER SHE DIES MY MOTHER TEACHES ME HOW TO SEW

The Egyptians say
that to speak of the dead
will bring them back to life

I call out her name
over and over
in the sadness of cities—

in all the places
she told me about—
the slaves

carrying the stones
building the pyramids—
the burning girls

jumping
from the sweat-shop windows
in New York City

and the workers' strike
in the Vilna
marketplace—

and then
the dark dark Polish forests
from which she did not return

I cut the cloth
hard on the table
the way she did
my hands move skilfully

so deftly
that I know they are not mine

her arms
fit into my sleeves
as she guides me—

a silver needle, a boat
skimming through the Euphrates
sews the garment

the way she wanted it

NIGHT-TIDE

All day we splinter.
Now something nudges us toward salt,
toward the pull of eelgrass.

Listen,
curlews are braiding the wind
into nests.

HITTING THE WALL

Woodpecker, black-and-white
downy, ladderbacked redcapped
male, now that the rolling
terror is over, wait,

as I waited this morning
after pushing myself through
too many miles in a valley
that trapped sun on the river road.

Soaked as though I had run
under the river,
I pushed myself uphill
to the point where a beached fish
panicked in my chest.

I have collared and dragged
the cat away, subtracting it
from your pulse rate. Let time
rest like a compress
on your forehead. We've been
to the edge today,
and seen the ground waiting.

Now there's the wisdom
of merely holding back, until fear
lies down in your breath
and your beak doesn't have to work
for air anymore.

I am with you, walking
each step of your runaway

heartbeat down, reliving
the morning. Don't fly!
Make time for the future's
drift from limb to limb. The way
this morning I eased myself
branch by branch
up the embankment. Here.

LEARNING THE TRADE

The surgeon I called for the dying trees
could fell a rotted elm with his head
hungover, he bragged with an accent
as Brooklyn as any bridge, could fell
the two I had with his eyes shut down.
I called him twice. The second time
a woman answered, her voice as rough
as locust bark, said the treeman had
broke down. I thought another thing.

I thought she meant the truck he used
had broken down, its axle wearied out
from root work, pulling up those dumb
drained mouths with nothing left to feed.
"No," she said again in a shout as if
I couldn't understand without the sound
of Brooklyn in my mouth. "No. Him.
He's broke down, blown a gasket. Done."
I went to see him for myself that fall.

His nerves sat around him like downed
power lines, loosed from responsibility.
His eyes earned their keep by shutting out
the risks he used to take to climb from there
to here. His arm twitched in its dead
socket, holding on to what was left for him
a couple hundred miles south of Brooklyn,
leaning into a high wind. Outside his house,
a rumpled sky raked up the emptied trees.

COUNTRY PLAY

The toy gun loads itself into his mouth.
He squeezes the day from his eyes,
what's left is an empty circle of sun,
paling like the early moon he saw
the night his father bled the pig.
These contradictions always make him sad,
though not enough to cry, enough to swell
inside him like his mother did that time
in pictures that he keeps upstairs.
The backdrop for this play is corn,
the green ears breaking like culs de sac
from the straight and narrow stalks,
and beans climbing like marines
up the perilous lattice strung between
two crutches left from when he broke
his foot, his only break before or since.
He has told the neighbor girl what he's
to do, has satisfied the cat, left cryptic notes,
and stands now in the heavy sun of afternoon,
his left hand pressed against his ear to kill
the sound. His trigger finger fondling the future
jerks and jerks again, practicing what's fatal
in this country scene, for later.

CATECHISM ELEGY

All night the long rain encloses the house
and I wake in quick confusion, as if the slow
winter wasp I'd seen inside the window last week
had stung my throat. I'm held in a dark hive
struggling to speak.

As deeply as years, around me you curve your parenthesis,
mother and father. Never far from you, or near,
even in dreams I listen for questions that gather

unnoticed. *Where are you? Where's your sister?*
Who are you? What have you done?

You taught me to love these questions like milk.
Daily I was to sound them, echo, and compel an inner life
so rich I'd pour through a hole in the cosmos,
a white river spilled from a source
still and invisible.

But they aren't the questions curved by your intimate
own pain, not the ones that curled their small
fists and knocked, asking in vain for breath
to unlock them.

These I heard at night when I'd stand
at the door of my room, listening.
I wasn't afraid of the dark,

only the sound of your breathing across the hall—
ragged, as if you struggled with an exacting
angel, a wrestling out of the ground
dark roots, or a sowing of stone.

I held back my longing to wake you.
What would you say?

                    And now, as the long rain circles
the house, I hear—as in sleep I hear dreams blow
against me like gusts of rain—your voices
wake me.

Whether they unfurl from the narrow solitude of death
or from the wider one of love, I cannot tell.
You ask me
What can you give? What have you abandoned?
For whom are you poor enough?

and I want to answer *death* to all three, to let the long
sight of it smooth and diminish
your discontent.
                    Isn't this what you want?

For the sting of death hummed in our daily bread,
it sweetened the coffee, it hemmed in the moment,
it sharpened the rude intent of our silence.

It was there, like a lemon held invisibly in your hands,
the only answer no one questioned,
a radiance that ripened.

THE WAYS

Soon the bats will fly into their endless cone of bouncing
back world. But not yet. They're packed like a black
taste on the roof of a mouth. And other of God's good,
strange (but actual) creatures are awake while we sleep
—Chinamen, for instance, that topsy-turvy people.
They bind feet. Their alphabet looks like little
houses in a row. The ways we take that original drug,
the cosmos, in and give it back is continual craziness
so common we call it life. The sheer hydraulic will
of a pine is worth a university's concentrated thought, its
cones are worth the totalled spasms of a whorehouse. Look
at it: deep black triangle silhouetted cleanly: *pine tree,*
look at it. It's hanging in your retina, in the dark there,
upside down, like a bat.

·

IMAGES OF THE SOUL

Because we think of it leaving the body at death,
somehow through the bone bars of its cage,

there's this chipped pottery bird, a teaspoon big,
they've excavated through layers of ancestors

down to the Neolithic—rib on rib, broke hip and
zigzagged skull, and this little flying thing from it.

Or: then why not this woolly mammoth
out from the heart of a glacier? The ice is melted

wholly now, but the mammoth is 200 kilograms.
It will last. It will come with a trumpet.

*

It will leap in recognition at the whistling
steam from a kettle, at the hum up

the invisible filament burning the visible
light in the tiny bulb-shape riding the wavering

bead of sweat across the belly dancer's flesh.
The idea of apple: in the seed: in the shit.

A word. The breath inside the word. The energy
in the breath. One hulking mammoth was found

with buttercups on its tongue, preserved completely.
At the moment of death: buttercups on its tongue.

When I Learn My Friend Must Lose Her Breast to Cancer

Remember the old fairytale?
A pea is placed under twenty
mattresses and twenty-eight
eiderdown quilts (the numbers
are quite exact). Perched
high on this nest of feathers
lies a real princess. She tosses
and turns all night. The moral
is not that pampered girls
cannot abide the coarser stuff
of life. No, the princess feels
the hard, round, immovable pea,
feels it intimately, knows its
dimensions. She senses what doesn't
belong, the imperfection bruising
her milk-white skin. Look you,
this is a true story.

*

When you draw the shape of the mass
they removed last week, I see a rat
with a tail, you see a sperm
swimming in your breast. You say,
"If this tumor has a name, its name
is Frank."

Darwin's mother told him when he was so young
he barely remembered, that if he looked deep
enough into a flower's center, that flower
would reveal its name.

Perhaps if I named my breasts, like I named
my children, I would care for them more,
be their proud mother.

*

At the Breast Screening Clinic
I meet Daphne, pink silicone model
with three implanted malignancies.
She teaches me what to search for
when I self-examine.

The mammogram reveals the aquamarine
subterranean world of breasts, an interlacing
network of rivers and streams. An outlaw
could find shelter here for weeks, even years.
Only the keenest arrow could flush him out.
Calcified deposits. Pebble in a granite bed.
Needle in a haystack. Anything suspicious.

But there is a startling beauty here,
a sheer blue expanse with darker
etched tracings. I think of coral
reefs seen through a blue filter.
And the sky blue ribs, like nothing
natural in their perfection: carved
blue ivory tusks. Whatever I am
looking at, it is foreign, pristine,
nothing that I care to touch.

The thermogram measures heat, explodes
in primary colors the breast we've sucked
as infants, violent in its reds
and greens. This is the breast of salt,
of blood, the one we could devour,
the one that could feed us.

*

I want to take away your guilt,
your belief that you are being
punished. "If I survive," you say,
"I will change my life." When I
was seven, I lost my bankbook,
prayed fervently to a benign
God leaning on His elbow,
taking a rest from thunder and other
people's prayers. "If you help me,"
I vowed, "I'll be a good girl forever
and ever." Even then I doubted my word.

I want to give you my white
satin nightshirt, the one
you love so much, with eyelet
at the throat and cuffs.
But you refuse: "I won't
be able to lift my arm."

*

At night I dream of my dead dog.
She wags her tail and drags a charred
useless limb. I try to hack it off,
filled with disgust at the gangrenous
smell. I'm afraid I will catch it,
I believe this in spite of myself.

*

"And how did you sleep last night?"
the princess was asked. "Oh quite
miserably! Goodness knows
what was in my bed. I am black
and blue all over." Then the Prince
took her for his wife, and the pea
was placed in a real museum

where it is to this day
unless somebody has carried it off.

*

PATH REPORT: ALL CLEAR

The word when it comes brings reprieve,
not a sentence. The head lifts up
off the chopping block, the neck
slips out from the noose, and a door
clanks shut on a world where a murder
of crows, a bright red mailbox, even
the cold gray sky, is miraculous.
"I will change my life," she'd said,
and the doctors came with their fancy
tools and cut the cancer away. Now
you see it, now you don't. Euphoria
lasted two days.

*

Dinnertime. Family scene. Two daughters,
a husband, a wife. The wife ladles soup
from a green tureen, one breast bobbing
in silicone splendor, the other drooping
its forty-two years. The daughters
squabble with sticks and stones, ignore
their mother's admonitions.

Enraged, suddenly, over what has spilt,
she pours a half-full glass of milk
down her elder daughter's budding chest.
Stricken, the girl flees to her room,
erects a barricade of chairs.
Her mother comes to blow it down.
And the house is made of wood.

◻ *Moishe Leib Halpern* ◻

(translated by Aaron Kramer)

BREAD AND FIRE

The sack is ready: rows of ripening rye unfurled—
enough for everyone who labors in the world.
But since it's gold the landlord barters for his rye,
empty in every poor man's house the sack must lie.
And since the villager has children to be fed
and since they're hungry and without one crust of bread—
it's not surprising that the man obeys his need
and comes to town and steals the bread on which you feed.
And since the golden showpiece that so brightly lies
across your belly cannot help but catch his eyes—
it's not surprising that he steals the chain as well.
Because of gold, his life has long since been a hell.
Because of gold, in fact, one time he even planned
to go at night and kill the owner of the land;
but since the landlord knows what dangers may befall,
a watchdog's in his yard, a sword is on his wall.

The axe is ready. Nice and sharp, but what's the good?
To chop down trees for everyone in need of wood.
But since the lord needs forests for his hunt, one must
put down the axe and leave it in the shed to rust.
And since the villager has children going bare,
and since the oven's ice, and not one log is there—
no wonder, Jew, that it's to you the man will come
and hack your door, your shutters down, to heat his home.
And, Jew, if you stretch forth your hand to stop the blade,
don't hope the man who swings the axe will give you aid.
And when you're lying on the ground, hands butchered, dead,
and when your blood along the ground runs fire-red—
no wonder if the man lifts back his weapon, Jew,
and, like a piece of timber, splits your head in two.
And since your screaming baby has a head, no wonder
if with one final blow he hacks the head asunder.

STILETTO

I knifed
my white Caddy
into the city
where I got fingered
as alternate juror
in an Hispanic murder case
that turned
on a blade's point
missing from the cops'
property room where,
evidently, evidence
moulders for decades until
mistrial, or appeal,
or disappears.
I listened hard although,
after concluding arguments,
unless one of my peers
took sick or was rubbed out,
I wouldn't be allowed
to speak, deliberate,
decide....

At lunch breaks, I pounded
pavement for time
to think, for danger
and shin-shivs I massaged
while in the jury box,
while all the while
that ubiquitous
fictional or real
blade-point kept
slipping between the ribs
of the accused, or,
alternately, the dead.
Tell me, Ramon Fernandez,

if you know, why,
after the last day after
my well-meaning conspirators
announced their verdict
to counter-pointed
threats, wails, sighs, why,
when I left the Hall of Justice,
I scraped a wrong turn
out of the parking lot
to yells and girders,
to car-horn and construction-crane
accompaniment that
parcelled out the sky
so asymetrically my
own perjurer's heart kept
thudding to testify
against God,
the absent landlord of these streets....

The judge pronounces sentence
maybe next week
from rows of books all
bound in neutral tones:
they, and he, usually
gavel down
the best they can, for order,
for community,
for justice so humanly
obscure, Ramon,
even guilty
defendants who can read
will cut pages
with their tongues and eye-teeth
to try to taste, to see.

In time, the prosecution
punctured all the dopeheads
who believed,

as they began to sing—
wonder of wonders—that they,
and we, are innocent
of free will, of all
but our own nature
suffused with circumstance....
I reached home,
my own dream
of hammock and trees
through which the sun,
as I lay gazing
into branchtips lost
in leaves, shone
like your earring
when you turned your face, Ramon,
burst into glare,
and blurred.

□ *David Hilton* □

THE OLD HOG FARM

Pinhole eyes burn white, caught
in the yellow reach of his flashlight—
then, squeals pitching higher, their fine
sandpapery scrape of nails clawing
toward him, down the rotten tin chute
where pig guts once quivered and slid.

Frozen prone, he's a hard skinny line
locking in the muzzle of his new .22.
The earth that holds him is solid, shaky
hogshit, offal, hogbrains, blood—
a century of slaughter turned under
and compacted a hundred strata deep.

But skulls can sometimes break
the crust, and glow above the muck.
He's seen one. It went in his sack, small
collection slowing the advance
of lawns, patios, mothers, dogs, morning
across his snake-rich, rat-rich tidal flats.

He doesn't have much time,
owls and bats already gone,
the hills behind Hayward just silvering,
and the wiry little cries now shrilling,
closing fast. He sights up a tunnel
of endless stench, and starts shooting.

WAR CORRESPONDENCE

He told me there are men who can do things
until your face becomes a thief you want
to execute. It says what they ask.
Tonight, the stars add nothing to the grass,
just these letters home, the names
and dates cut neatly out. A child,
I held them to a lantern in the kitchen,
peeking through the blanks. I knew
he cried, my mother standing dockside,
San Francisco, harbor lights disappearing.
I had not been born, then, imagine him
as something in her arms left out.
Later, he had only three more things
to say: the head a soldier wedged
into the grill on his green Jeep,
the Mess Hall where the G. I.'s dumped
their food in pails that kids held
through the wires, and pilots screaming,
late at night, in the field hospital,
lights coming on in the hot compound.
He says it seems like hours before they stopped.
It didn't stop. And who can think of history
for long? Too small, kindness, a bit of cloth
against a broken lip, and then the onionskin,
snipped and littering a censor's wooden floor.
What's left of his horror but this?
To take the thin letters up again, remember
how it was. To put my hand behind the page,
my fingers to the holes. To let the light
come, again, through where my father lived.

NOTEBOOK

Do some simple things…do the arms
and legs of a dancer, or the small
of her back, do her shoes …Degas

Do the ones you've scribbled down
in your head, the ones at the stoplights,
lunch counters,
the ones at the bus stop,
the ones in your bed.
Do the ones you underlined,
the ones scraping
like dry brushes,
the ones that whisper:
listen, hold on now, just wait.

And if they don't come out
at once from your silence,
flapping and beating their wings,
caught in your smell of surprise,
another, just a hint of shape,
will fly up right past your eyes.

And from whatever it is that shakes out
the dice of our dreams,
whatever chemicals or cells bonding
or a song that's too low to be heard,
some feathers, nest-makings will fall away
gliding down to your simple beginnings.

□ *Jean Janzen* □

EVERY YEAR THE BODIES

Every year the bodies
are dragged from the lake,
boys becoming men
testing the water a little
too far, their deaths
looking so much like play.
Rescuers think
that they have found them,
but their split youth
has escaped, searching
the summer skies for a shape,
a place to be.
And every spring the dam
opens once again,
water explodes
over the concrete and steel,
and on the leaning hillsides,
poppies, snowdrops and lupine
stand upright, breathing.

TROUT RUN

A Poem for Death in Seven Movements

for John and Helen Clendenin

(1)

Coming Back in Autumn

Outside the yellow cave my headlights made,
something stirred. But people who know this road
learn to forgive dark things the light can't find;
they'll forgive my ignoring what might have lit up
on the walls of that cave the way they've forgiven
some sad long night of their own when the river
had no stars. Up here in Trout Run, Steam Valley,
they know how light held under ice this time of year
makes little fists that strike far south of here
like cold stars pounding rocks in the river's mouth.

So they learn to let go the light. I also try
to let go. Go gentle, I want to say—but first
my hands and eyes must clench to grasp what it means
to catch: to see, to fix in the mind, to snag
on barbs, to hold a leap as of breadth, to stop
the drift of shapes. Well, then, of autumn, of endings,
for dying: all we can string home from the river.

(2)

Waking at Clendenin's

In morning light, only the thin
pane of glass can keep the frost
and bloodlit trees on one side,

steam of tea and Verdi on the other.
The mist that ragged the hills at dawn
takes down its flags. Inside,
splinters of red and bronze
drive into the spines of upright books.

There is a way to live
by these exchanges of light:
mountains and books in this house
have neighborly words together:
the daughter Lucinda's mythic name
ignites into *Tinda* while Verdi
catches the hues of those leaves,
finding the mathematics of stars.

* * * * * *

Last night the sky was all the sound
there was. Its tone was dark.
The owl forgot to take in his black sails
so hawks and other minds, red and brash
old hunters, were waiting in blinds.
I woke to a change in key out there,
muted like the front-room window glass
turning bluer each fall toward snow.

I thought the sound might be
the feet of deer who steal down
to the lawn and step onto moonlight,
or stones being rubbed in the stream
or stars in trees. But nothing unhuman
trembles like that. Beyond dry leaves
are whispers, old lovers, old names.

I know last summer's shade trees wait
in cold with their long, meat-eating roots.

(3)

Stranger in the Village

Walking, they say in this house, is good: it smokes the scotch.
I walk the streets of Trout Run in the lurid disguise
of the Stranger. A schoolboy on a bike rides next to me
and asks where I'm going. O just walking, I say,
just walking all over the streets of this old town.
He does not believe me. So now I have him:
now whatever truth I say off-hand will be to him
some flash of legend. He asks me where I'm from.
I shrug. From fairly far away, I say; just came in
from Michigan—and I hook my thumb over the mountains, west.
He winks and grins as though I've told him Pluto.
Now we are friends. How far are you going?
O just to the end of some final street, then back—

and now like a boy encountering some mad Jesus
but trusting, he suddenly stops his weaving bike.
Who are you? he asks. That question older than fire
for which I am never ready. To what can I witness?
I am the piper without a pipe, Adam looking for home—
all this truth tricks me to say I'm a poet—as though
that's still an occupation. And then the boy reaches back
for some tribal voice as old at least as his mountains.
He hooks his thumb toward the end of the street.
At the hotel, he says, they'd probably give you a beer, for free.

(4)

The Loving Shape of Disorder

It's the kind of afternoon
you'd like to nap in the attic
drowsing under the shuffle and knock of wind.
But we three walk instead
to Bryan Rudge's farm
just up the little road along the stream
where chairs and fruitjars sing like Methodists.
At eighty-five he holds and clips
a formal garden on a shelf, part way up
John's mountain, above the line of the roof.
Bushes and trees are clipped to be
Italian fountains, pairs of lanterns;
everything tries old clapping of hands
to say with art, *remember we are here.*
Darker down in his yard where he legends himself,
two ice-cream-cone trees stand stiff,
circled with painted bowling pins.
From the front window sill a radio
saws its lock-step rhythm over the wind.
Dark is on the way, and snow,
and Bryan Rudge, who trims out every word
and can name us every track and plant
the length of Steam Valley, and up,
probably thinks he works alone
at taming the mountain and carving the human in.
But the shaping of Eden is out of control.
In a spray-painted bush that hints of fire,
hubcaps hang from plastic fishing line.
Coming back down, two of us talk of primitive art
while one-half remembers a garden he left long ago.

(5)

The Winter I Didn't Come Up

A good cold morning
has the startled eye of a bird.
Cold sings tunes to bones,
somebody said, and I know
the cells in your bones
are out of control and even
the singing by now must ache.
I clap the bird away
and wish you a day when that riot
of cells will ring and beat
and pull and swing like bells
so hard the day will forget to turn
while you listen like a child
for the end and you nod away
to night inside the ringing.

(6)

Last Spring

When I was a child, I knew one thing
for sure: I knew what glory meant:
glory was the dance of bits of dust
in a beam of sunlight pointing to our rug.

John, your good eye gone, you make the bad eye
good, or make it do. You sharpen another sight
past sight, a mind out there in the violet dark
of empty space with which you watch the dance of dust.

The only thing you'd wave a placard for, you said,
was benevolent anarchy. Trying your sight
I watch it come again. It opens and shuts
like chickory, not like a fist. It's spring.

While light comes pointing to lights
the flowers have banked all winter long
birdsong falls out of trees
and again the dew has stained our pantlegs

high up the thighs while we wade a morning
and talk of what the proper work should be
in a point-on-the-map named Buttonwood, PA:
Stitching. Tinkering. Bottling nut-brown ale.

John, last spring is three days past.

(7)

Autumn Was Home

There's trouble in the valley
but it's only the world's,
nothing we or the village can fix,
trouble as old as knife or moon.
If sticks and stones tell tales on us,
the tales are only remote—
like what astronomers tell on stars.

My eye stays home. In this old house
two friends weave life and thought
by what they call "collecting a quiet center."
The roads by which they came
slowly die behind, under leaves.
Leafstorms—a favorite word in this word-drunk house—
smother Trout Run like the river in blazes

of fractured lights. The dream we walk in
always drifts out of control in its dreamy way.
So almost certainly this legend, this place
we shape will fall again, run off some night

with those reckless boys the lights
of neighboring towns that come riding down
to shoot up the streets of Trout Run in our sleep.

But it is never time to fly.
Plotinus is wrong: the material world is not
a sinking, a failure of wing. It's home.
Night and snow are what happens
to unify the world (we name the rhythm death)
before the boozy birds out there
can start it up again, its holy clamor,

darkness made us talk with harder words,
pain is how the stones catch hold
of the harmony of stars
and maybe it is enough
to have caught the catch of light
all we could string
home from the river.

DRIFTING

I saw the hand of Rasputin
cast in bronze and used as an oversized
paperweight on someone's desk.
The authentic hand. Smooth as Italian leather.
It was molded from plaster before he was killed.
Bought at an auction in Europe.
She was a collector.
She knew the value of everything.

I wouldn't like Rasputin's hand
on my desk, even though it wore the skin
over its fine bones like a soft glove
and healed the tsarevitch.
I wouldn't like her samurai sword.
I'm glad I don't know what I'm worth.

There are days when the whole world
feels like somebody else's collection.
Even your hands. We walk
in another country and the mist
slowly rises above the lake
like all the heaviness we left,
dissolving.
Only it's not our heaviness.

*

Sometimes, waking, I forget
where I am. The things around me
go on with their old existence
like props in a play, as if the curtain
has just risen on a room in an Italian villa.
It's not my play.

In the old life there was a photo

of Valentino on my desk.
Agnes Ayers was swooning in his arms,
the Sheik in a rapture of lips
without any words.

Benevolent uncles spoke in a language
I didn't know, their fleshy hands,
their anxious eyes smiling
as they patted me gently on the head.
Like watching a silent movie,
when they opened their mouths
like fish under water
I turned off the sound.

All that sweet absence.

*

Once I learned the thirteen principles
of Rabbi Salanter, but I remember
only seven: truth, diligence, honor,
repose, cleanliness, frugality,
and silence. If I collected words
they would have to belong,
like moss or fleas. Things you say
that I can believe in.

Honor reminds me too much of the Samurai.
I like repose. It belongs to this landscape
where even the lizards rest
when we stand still
and look at the wall together.

Naming the things of this world
you begin to own them.
Cyclamen. Mustard.

□ *Shirley Kaufman* □

I can't manage so many flowers.
But I already know the word for lake in Italian.

*

Gulls wheel over Lago di Como
at sundown on their way south
trying to catch the last warm currents.
Their wings are white, then silver, and then smoke
when the light abandons them
and dusk settles in their feathers.

If you don't collect things,
it's easier to move. Easier to stand
on this cliff for another minute
and watch the leaves fall, one by one,
yellow, into the lake.
They belong to the air
for the time they are drifting.
It's a long way down.

STRANGE TEMPTATION

His smell is here; among flourescent lights,
industrial fixtures and the traffic hum
outside these modern walls and down six floors.

I opened the door. A smell of musk and dust
and something else. I saw the snake who lived
in Charly's closet, stretched across the shelf
and down the wall, dry paper tongue made real.
I didn't know he had one. A snake, I mean.

A friend of Charly's said he knew I was
a girl who wanted more. He knew the truth,
but I was vague on what wanting's all about.

He had no name. And Charly was nameless, too,
before he found the Lord and me. He prayed
for courage not to touch me but we failed.
The friend breathed fire when he spoke of strange
temptations, blowing rings. Of smoke, I mean.

The smell is here as time folds in on me.
His smell, or is it Charly's, or the snake's
or my sweat on the basement bedroom floor?

And stumbling in the Saviour's arms, seduced
by a promise of forgiveness, we forgot
the truth. The other spoke, and in my haste,
embracing strange temptations, I became
the apple that I am. Myself, I mean.

QUARTER TO SIX

Quarter to six
and the house swept with the colors of dusk
I set the table with plates and lace.
In these minutes left to myself
before the man and child scuff at the doorstep
and come in, I think of you and wonder
what I would say if I could write.
Would I tell you how I avoid his eyes, this man
I've learned to live with, afraid of what
he doesn't know about me. That I've finished
a pack of cigarettes in one sitting, to ready myself
for dinner, where my hands will waver over a plate
of fish as the bones of my daughter grow normal
in the chair beside me. Missy

this is what's become of the wedding
you swore you'd come to wearing black. That was in 1970
as we sat on the bleached floor of the sanitarium
sharing a cigarette you'd won in a game of pool.
You said even school was better than this ward
where they placed the old men in their draped pants,
the housewives screaming in loud flowered shifts
as they clung to the doors that lined the halls.
When we ate our dinner of fish and boiled potatoes
it was you who nudged me under the table
when the thin man in striped pajamas
climbed the chair beside me in his bare feet, his pink
tinged urine making soup of my leftovers.
With my eyes locked on yours I watched you
keep eating. So I lifted my fork to my open
mouth, jello quivering green against the tines,
and while I trusted you and chewed on nothing
he leapt into the arms of the night nurse
and bit open the side of her face. You had been there

longer, knew the ropes, how to take
the sugar coated pill and slip it into the side pocket
of your mouth, pretend to swallow it down in drowsy gulps
while the white frocked nurse eyed the clockface above our heads.
You tapped messages into the wall while I wept and struggled
to remember the code, snuck in after bedcount with cigarettes,
blew the blue smoke through barred windows. We traded stories,
our military fathers, yours locking you in the closet for the days
it took to chew ribbons of flesh from your fingers, your dresses
piled into a bed—then mine, who worked his ringed fingers
inside me while the house slept, my face pressed
to the pillow, my fists knotted into the sheets. Some nights

I can't eat. The dining room fills
with their chatter, my hand stuffed with the glint
of a fork and the safety of butter knives
quiet at the sides of our plates.
If I could write you now I'd tell you I wonder how long
I can go on with this careful pouring of the wine from its bottle,
straining to catch it in the fragile glass.

Tearing open my bread I see the scar,
the stitches laced up the root of your arm, the flesh
messy where you grabbed at it with the broken glass
of an ashtray. That was the third time. And later you laughed
when they twisted you into the white strapped jacket, demanding
you vomit the pills. I imagined you in the harsh light
of a bare bulb where you took
the needle without flinching, retched
when the Ipecac hit you, your body shelved over the toilet
and no one to hold the hair from your face. I don't know

where your hands are now, the fingers
that filled my mouth those nights you tongued me open
in the broken light that fell through chicken wired windows.
The intern found us and wrenched us apart, the half moon
of your breast exposed as you spit on him.

"Now you're going to get it," he hissed
through his teeth and you screamed "Get what?"
as if there was anything anyone could give you.
If I could write you now I'd tell you.

    I still see your face, bone white as my china
above the black velvet cape you wore to my wedding
twelve years ago, the hem of your black crepe skirt
brushing up the dirty rice in swirls
as you swept down the reception line to kiss me.

    "Now you're going to get it," you whispered, cupping
my cheek in your hand.

□ *Barbara F. Lefcowitz* □

SARABANDE

Death broke into my mother's bedroom at 3 a.m.
speaking such rapid Spanish
she could not respond in any known tongue;
beckoned him closer with an ice-blue finger
to make sure he was not
a common thief, bent on lifting her wedding ring,
melting its gold for his treasury.

He vanished with the grace of a toreador,
many rounds to make tonight, many rounds.
Five days before he could return, lift
her twisted tissue-thin body, *Ay Caramba!*
and for a blink she was Carmen Miranda
performing the Mexican Hat Dance, then
once again floating in pools of gardenias and orchids,
Puerto Vallarta, 1950.

Or so I like to think,
kicking open for a blink
doubt's iron gates, sinking
into the long forbidden pool of childhood,
where every pebble was a miracle
and it would have been easy to believe
that when she lay five days in a coma
she must have dreamed
of Spain's red earth, García-Lorca, Goya,
El Greco, Segovia;
of dancing with them an elegant sarabande,
her red polka-dot 1940s playsuit
blending with the blood-suffused soil of Andalusía,
dancing slowly but inexorably
towards what I would like
to call Paradise
but can only call memory.

METAPHOR

When metaphor speaks, she can say anything.
She is yellow dressing up as a whore
or a socialite. She is your hair a soft avalanche of rain;
light undressing herself and rising on fiery impulses of red.
She is your tongue like a humming bird or your palms
lifting sound from its sleep or storms raising
their hands in truce. Metaphor is in love with anything.
With small hills recalling mountains of memory.
Here she is, now, escorting you to the dinner
you were not invited to. She smiles as if you were the one love
in her life. The room glows with applause.
Metaphor is at your service. *Always*, she says
and then adds, just don't take me for granted. I am no
sentimental blonde. I have an accountant.
I pay my bills on time. Metaphor knows her needs
and yours—she charges accordingly. Nothing is free,
she says and means it. When you have become too comfortable
metaphor will knock on your door bearing cut flowers
as if to say, *beautiful like us, yes,*
but how long can they survive? Metaphor will walk into your house
as if she were your double. She will begin
mourning death in the most elaborate tropes—
she will speak of delicious grief, the sweet pain of sorrow,
the parting of love like rivers. All the lights in your father's house
are off forever, she says. Metaphor lacks propriety.
Nothing is too much for her, or too little—she is insatiable,
forgets civility, rises in passionate anger. Just when you take her
for a friend, confessing everything, baring your nakedness
metaphor grabs hold of you like a mad cop and roughs you up.
Why you ask? For the hell of it, she replies.
Count on nothing, she says, and throws you out into the dark.
Find your own way back, she calls. I may be the arm on your
    shoulder.
Or the flood in your heart. Or the absence you back into.

THE PERSISTENCE OF POLYTHEISM

1. Aphrodite

The riffraff at the ballpark
died away.
She walked like a queen
out of nowhere
to the first baseman.
He touched his cap's blue bill.
The ball in his glove was gold.
His glove was like a sunset.
Everybody felt her lips.

2. Hermes

Shrewd and tricky, like skating
with your eyes closed: he comes
with a shadowed hiss.
You are there, but your words
are slippery and tripping.
I swear wings
made my tongue say run
instead of home.
The moon held her silver belly.

3. Pan

She'll never come back,
you know that now.
All the leaves have eyes.
The tent is miles away,
and the path is branching off
to disappearing tracks.
Your heart is like a clown's
red balloon about to pop.
You try to laugh
but the trees are on fire.

All the leaves have eyes
and call you fool.

                                                    4. Hades

The world's last gentleman,
picking flowers.
He was bowing to us, old world,
but we couldn't see him.
A girl on a tricycle
was wheeling down the street.
Her mother was inside,
watching t.v., who knows?
It was late September,
red wet leaves.
The car had no driver.

FROM THE SERIES "LETTERS BACK: GOD WRITES TO EMILY DICKINSON"

*

Why, when I speak to myself,
do I so often think of you?
You've hardly seen the world,
while I contain it. And yet
when my net flies out, settles
in a hush over the river,
you're the one who never
feels trapped, who knows
how to weave
in and out of that mesh.

I like having you on the earth,
a reminder that what I give there,
so often misconstrued, is felt
in one who could not be my wife
or sister, but walks
the labyrinth of my love
as if she had a map.

Construction (II)

Around the city in thousands of places
they are mixing sand, water, gravel, cement
and making concrete, pouring it into forms,
buildings are rising, harmonic and functional,
steel and glass, wires, cables, concrete, wood,
and in them people will be sitting, sleeping,
eating, making up stories, listening,
falling in love, alone and helpless and falling in love,
avid and lovely falling in love, the stupid
and the winsome falling in love, they are taking
their clothes off, flesh and flesh meet softly,
meet with cries, meet just in time,
he enters, they conceive, a new person is born,
corn grows, more corn grows, mouths eat,
books are written, in thousands of places
people praise the lord, people walk up stairs,
dustpans are emptied, in thousands of places
trash piles up, is squashed down,
they make parks, houses are built, bushes grow,
we walk back and forth, holding hands,
thinking about poems, thinking about love,
loving, making something new, making something big,
planning a building, planning for happiness,
picking a book off the shelf, reading,
changing our mind, yes, to love you is possible,
you will love me, if you don't
I will love you regardless, changed,
never to be lonesome again loving you so much,
after all, we have made something new, something
strange, there are flowers blooming, and in the jungles
birds and monkeys, the rivers slowly sliding along,
full of nutriment.

After Eden

We never see them
in the same place twice.
Sometimes in cold weather
we find them sunning

like old men in Miami,
or coiled between roots
of junipers, giving shade
a bad reputation.

If we see them uncaged,
we stumble upon them
swimming still water,
fleeing through grass

like a whisper,
or down on their bellies
in hardscrabble
scraping their scales clean

across flint and hot sand,
rattle tip-up and bitter,
searching for anything better,
anywhere without people.

Deciduous

Every autumn grackles circled
the tree. Did they wonder
plums? plums? No plums were
revealed to them. The tree was,
after all, ornamental.
Only red leaves fell,
and what might have been plum
was cardinal.
    One year, though,
in no haste, a brown beetle
stuck itself to the tree
and shrugged off its husk.
Birds and people hurried by,
taking no notice of anything
beetlish, but a small girl
found the winged carapace,
held it to her finger
like a birthstone. That very night
she dreamed of leaving home.

SMALL GREASEFIRE IN THE KITCHEN

Here fire and water daily are made mild.
Here mess gets made and then comes clean.
Water dozes in these pipes like dazed sap;
the pilot light, that bud, won't bloom
unless he turns his wrist. He runs this place.

And yet one night he sears some lamb for stew,
some lambfat spurts into the flame,
some on his hand—then a blue cuff wavers
around his wrist until he snuffs
it with a towel. To eat is no small

business, accomplice to fire admits.
He looks quite idiomatic
in an apron, but isn't he the boy
from the cartoons with sulky eyes
and a chemistry set, just grown up some?

□ *José Antonio Mazzotti* □

(translated by G. J. Racz)

MARE IS THE FEMALE OF THE HORSE

(after an essay by Roman Jakobson)

Mare is the female of the horse and *mare*
is my woman, unpronounceable the rest of my days,
      her cool
sweat and cool hard hooves like teeth
and her back on which I ride surrounded by shrap-
      nel and sirens that precede a heavy bombing.

Mare is the female of the horse and *mare* is my woman
with her gentle neigh of a hundred violins four flutes two
      trumpets
and a forgotten bleary-eyed music, stubble-laden, on
      lonely nights.

She moves through the parks swelling her haunches
      (as I swell my lungs)
she leaps and kicks and is not acquainted with passionless men
she bares a smile as someone opening a sack of
      rice
knows and does not know, feels and does not feel,
      shouts and does not shout,
and showers the newlyweds with rice.

Mare is the female of the horse and *mare* is my woman,
      an unpronounceable
and divine metalanguage I can pronounce but not embellish
I leap and kick and neigh and follow no more
I know that she will come like a tasty morsel to forgive me
      these words.

GRANDFATHER AT THE POOL

Now that I'm old
respectable and white and pink
you tease like bold
hotblooded courtesans who think
old men prefer thin beer to drink

But I could take
the whiskey of your lips and eyes
and still not slake
this thirst for brandy-colored thighs:
this the dead end of growing wise

The bubble in
our blood will boil and sing: the heart
has never been
a dry bright and studious part
but in dark chambers plies its art

So let it be
that youngsters at this sunny pool
have sport with me
and set me dancing like a fool:
we have milleniums to cool

RURALS

The Rekindling

At eight the widowed postmistress
opens the cash-box. She counts
specie and bills. Same as yesterday.
She breathes on them
until they glow as bright
as when she banked their fires for the night.
Now she can issue stamps.

The fat body

of the '54 Buick
in the junk-yard in the hollow
contains chromed music.
Voices flaking rust
sing from a box under the dash-board,
under St. Christopher, now a legend,
under the frozen necker's knob.
Dinah, Bing, they moan
to a pool of rainwater from the later '70s
collected in rubber hollows on the floor
from clouds that were great beauties in their day.

Single Standard

He said: I suppose nobody has worked
harder at love than I have.
I mean, no one has tried
to give more, to more

and she: there was
in the town where I grew up
a similar character,
the town whore.

□ *Leonard Nathan* □

Them

The ones with the still and remote faces,
who smile sometimes but aren't happy,
frown sometimes but aren't disappointed,
who have said goodbye long before separation,
who look unflinching at the glory
of the almond tree in blossom,
or at black distance without stars
to relieve it—they are the ones
who know just when and how
and perhaps why, the ones
I watch for signs.

When they pack and leave
I pack and leave. When they sigh
and stay I stay.

They are like experienced waiters
who see it all in a glance, who know
their job and never confuse it
with serious business, who remember
what the occasion needs and wait
till they're called for to do what's required
with no fuss and the few right words.

They are like ex-priests
who still can give the lost directions
for another world but have chosen this one
because it demands all their faith
just to remain human.

To them the outburst of the almond
is only another timely diversion

already foreseen in the cold necessity
of December when the tree stood there
naked of all but essentials.

To them we are like children
begging for a good story
or the trick of disappearing coins.
They listen patiently to our babble
but never take their eyes off the door.

WASTE

The glittering burial mound of flattened cars,
Some of them spattered inside with blood,
And on the other side of the soaring bridge
On the way to the airport, the cracking plants,
Tall silver candles flaming at their tips
While they refine the fuel of fresh desires—

Riding between petroleum and rust
To rise above our little lives awhile
And see the cities and the parking lots
From high above as the gods used to do,
Or as cryptic patterns made of beaded lights,
An everlasting Christmas tree of life—

Till the aircraft meets its shadow once again
And we are as we were, in another town
Not much unlike the one we thought we had left,
Ourselves the same selves we had left behind
Reduced again into the plane of love
And fear and all-obligatory guilt—

There is no end to the loves we flew to meet,
The funerals duty bound us to attend
At energies that never were till now
And quivering anxieties also new
In their pitch of tension and discontent
And impatience to be getting there, but where?

Now in the taxi into town we pass
Again, as if it were another life
Reviewed, the heaped up mass of rusting cars
And on the other side of the soaring bridge
The cracking plants, the candles of desire
That lead us on to unconsidered ends—

Our destinations being destinies,
Because we lust and fear and worry about
Our lust and fear and what the future holds
For us who waste the world while doing time,
Making the babies, attending the funerals,
Cutting the deals, catching the next flight out.

◻ *Jean Nordhaus* ◻

WOOD

for Peter & Shirley

Once begun
it's an obsession.
You become this hunt

and where innocent
benches stood, and trees,
you now see fire
in a 2x4, in cast-off shingles
harbored heat, prose
in driftwood

trailing it
like a still green limb
to make a home for heartbreak
under the stair, cozen
from derelict objects
their music:

logs by a streetlamp
asleep in the salt
of their snoring,
bones of a bed, a whale
washed up on grass,
a bent guitar.

Wood is good
is homely, dull
is gray or brown
is all around, and though it
may not sound like brass
or even chime,

these unexpected finds
will warm you
in the long nights coming.

THE CREATURE

Without thinking, I drop my notebook
square on the fly the size of a tiny
mammal, there on the floor. Only as I
watch, from above, the great, fluttering
roof descend, do I understand
I am killing. Solid papery splat,
three-section spiral, sky-blue—I
pick it up and find nothing. The dark
miniature fatted calf of the fly
untaken! Later I see it on its side
under the edge of the bureau. It stretches a
barbed leg, slowly, out
the way my father's leg on its own would
stiffen when he was dying, he'd bare the
innards of his mouth, it would run down
slowly from the corners, the river of white clay.
I kneel to the creature. Its broad back is
olive striped with black, its eyes
coral balls, its anus a small
coral bead. Elegantly,
the tip of the stretched limb begins to
beat time, bending at the wrist,
silky, single-fingered hand
tapping. It can never come back from this.
I have seen stunned flies leap
and sail away, but not when they've gone
over this far into the lyrical—
smashed by a book of first drafts. And yet not
smashed, the abdomen is flawless,
scaled like an aster calyx—it coughs
twice, hump, hump, I lay my
cheek on the floor beside it the way I
rested my head on the bed beside my father in the
path of his last breaths, they came
forth, spiral beasts of air

from his mouth, and from the back of his throat
meteor dust. Grain by dark
grain, feathery barb by barb the
fly uncurls a leg, another, then,
joints undone, a woman in labor,
rises, stands, shudders, then in a
sudden rush runs three light steps and
throws itself over on its back. Nothing,
nothing, then a voluptuous stretching of its
four unsevered legs, then
a rapid delicate paddling in the air
and I realize I should kill it. I would have killed
my father if he'd asked. I always wanted
some large violent act with him.
And he died like a *flower*, drying out, turning color,
adding those black oval flecks to his eyeballs.
Before I crush it I go close to the fly and for the
first time, I notice its wings,
translucent, veined with amber, they are like petals.
Nothing of them remains from the crushing.
Just wads of dark like earth, and behind it,
on the paper, a bloom of dust and blood.
I look at it and look at it.
Seeing has taken in me the place of love,
and radiates, and almost fills it.

The Morning after Kristallnacht
(November 7, 1938)

The Germans gather in front of the store, they
peer in, the tips of their chic
shoes at the lip of a pool, swimmers who have
not yet worked up the nerve to wade in—
glass broken into slub, knobs,
muzzles, strips, faceting-slag in a
heap under the windows. Their hair
curled in stiff ridges, like the coats
of commercial sheep, the ladies look down at the
glass crushed to its molecules and
smeared. A few, huge spears of
pane remain in the gaps of the shop-front,
weapons that have not been lifted yet, but
otherwise there is nothing but dazzling
ruin, the shoppers gaze at it, as
if any minute they'll take off their shoes and go
in, step right down, into
the glazed street of Berlin, into the
stone, its dark, heavy water, and swim.

THE GIFT

No one is waiting. No one watches
the mist and few stars as they gather.
Somehow you are the only one to see
the rain as it starts.

You have learned to love the late hour,
the detail of stillness
—everything the color of rain in darkness.

In an hour, the pale moon will mean nothing
more than morning and an equally blank sky.
It offers you nothing. I give you this.

Something simple, ordinary,
something you might learn to fear.

SONG

I am sick of the song
of the self,
that old melody
for one voice
running up and down
and up the scale
like a mouse maddened
by its own elusive
tail. I have heard that voice
shatter glass.

Nor do I ask
for martial music,
trumpets or drums
or the thoroughbass
of marching feet.
I long, instead, for bells
or for a simple trio: one bird
in the sycamore singing,
two birds in the oak
singing back.

□ *Linda Pastan* □

BY THE MAILBOX

The message you send me
is silence. It is a message
I try to understand
the way the roots
of trees must understand
the mitigating silence of water.
We take from nature
what we can. I study
the silences of stars, of stones.
I picture you miles north
leaning over the empty page.
Dear . . . you want to write.
But already the page is a window
curtained in the early silence
of snow.

PISTACHIOS

To the two who have denied themselves
the pleasures they can now afford:
to the father who picks glass
out of a dropped peanut butter jar,
foraging to make a sandwich;
to the mother shopping downtown
for a cheap but passable wig;
to them with over fourteen decades
of scrimping between them,
human grease on dollar bills
wrapped in rubberbands, their budget
figured down to the thin music
of dimes, the department store
basement underwear (how does it fit
in the crotch?), pawed-over bargains,
yellowed t-shirts off irregular looms,
bus rides in the rain, the diesel
fumes coming up under the seats,
to those two I bring the fat figs
of California, candy brittle—just
sugar, almonds and butter,
and finally nuts, the kind of which
they've never tasted, not the pink
imports dyed garish like teenagers
in neon jackets, but blond shelled
green-meated pistachios, an entire
five-pound sack of pleasure, which
they balk at like animals offered
new food, but a handful into them
they stop talking and just eat,
empty husks dropping like pennies
into a beggar's cup, and I tell them
about artichoke hearts crowded in jars
the size of lampshades, mustard clinging

with dill and French sunshine, of a lazybones
intermittent gluttony they can acquire now
and then, a heedless supper followed by
a demitasse of blithesomeness.

☐ *Richard Peabody* ☐

SHE DISCOVERS JAZZ

stumbles over it
    more likely

purloined letters

as though love
is spelled

wynton

and jazz
something
that never existed

your records
invisible
all those years

a moon
whose gravity
she refused to obey

until his ears

more interesting
than yours

heard

what she
was trying
to say

CAPE MISERY

The dogs are blown from their harnesses.
We ourselves (six men have gone ahead)
are flung on our faces.

We shoulder the sledge
call the affrighted dogs
and reach the rocks of Eider Island.
The air swirls and darkens.
We must sledge ahead or perish.

The snow overwhelms, roofs,
and quilts us under.
Far outside, a remote thunder.
The wind's a great fly-wheel.
Snow hails upon the surface
of our natural hut.
The canopy collapses.

Twenty hours later, forty
miles of floundering, we reach
the others on the floes.
Thank God, their ice still holds.

□ Mary Quattlebaum □

THE STATUE SPEAKS WITH PYGMALION

You're proud of this brute
stone you hoaxed
into breasts and thighs
and of my crisp,
vermiculate
curls.
See how shadows
coil
in curves and pits,
those hollows
your two thumbs
contrived.

And now
this unnatural
act:
my scraped bones
stunned and shaking
into flesh.

Already the ivory
egg slips
and plummets
into my core's
ripe
parabola, and thickens
the child
who holds the boy
who will love too well
his own creation.

The curling shadows lengthen.
This boy grows
imperious, cold;

but, oh, his daughter
is treated like a queen!
See her gowns and little shoes,
the rich jewels that blush
against her chest.
See how he strokes and strokes
her body
into something beautiful
and stone.

THE DREAM

In my dream two chestnut horses
Were pulling a plow,
My grandfather chiding them
As though he must
Have forgotten that he had turned
Long since to dust.
It is said that a dream dissolves
In seconds. Yet
I watched until those two
Horses were silken with sweat.

How an Older Man Makes Love

Not as if seeing Jupiter through a telescope
and, holding his breath transfixed, he marvels
at his first heavenly body, orbital
and unclothed. Nor
as a boy who leans out from a train gathering speed
and tries to face the wind, but its strength
tears his eyes and the birds, the flowers
whizzing past are a kaleidoscopic blur. No.
                                        Realizing
timing is everything, an older man polishes
the same smooth stone. The country of strawberry
skin is safe in his patient hands
as his dusty breath shuffles in and out
from the warm nest of his lungs. Each
valley and fold help him remember
where he has been, which faint scent to follow
next, and I have to admire how friendly
shadows collect, slightly wavering, almost ready.
When he is tired he rests, knowing to hurry
is to fail because anywhere
is the same familiar place he has returned to
again and again. Through shutters
his cry exfoliates summer gone from the trees.
A blue vein over softening bone—
I kiss his pulse.

Fate, Like Jayne Mansfield, Takes a Road Trip

I. Fate Binds Man and Man Submits

Houdini-like, he steps into the brass trunk
with great bravado, a show of hands,
lights flashing, cymbals crashing.
The woman binds the trunk with chains.
They are heavy chains, gold-plated chains
snatched from the necks
of innocent tourists. She bows deeply, gravely,
to the crowd and then she seals the trunk
with chewing gum. The woman's name is Faith
but she is called Fate for short.
Fate seals the trunk,
then opens the trunk of her white gleaming Cadillac.
The strong man helps her load the brass trunk
into the other trunk. You are holding cotton candy
and watching, you are watching all this
from the great iron spiderweb of the ferris wheel.
You cannot believe it. You are in love with the man,
the Houdini in the trunk. He is not an escape artist,
he is not very mechanically inclined,
he doesn't even know how to change the oil
in his car. Fate is his mother
and she is driving away with him.
He is your lover and he is bound and gagged,
chained into a brass trunk, riding away
in the trunk of a Cadillac.
You are watching the lights of the carnival as you rise
closer to the night sky. You keep thinking to yourself *escape, escape.*

II. Fate Takes Man for a Ride

When we last left our hero he was bound and gagged,
but he had stepped into a big brass trunk like Houdini—
don't forget his bravado. His mother, a platinum blonde named Fate,

had chained the trunk closed and locked the brass trunk
into the trunk of her new white Cadillac. Off she sped into the sunset,
looking for all the world like Jayne Mansfield, the car roof down,
a long white scarf fluttering in the wind, a cigarette dangling
from her Passion Red lips. Now the man is lying in a fetal position
in the trunk. He doesn't know his destination, but he fancies Florida,
maybe Miami, Florida's little toe. He is thinking *oranges,*
alligators, pink shorts. Fate is speeding down the long expressway
towards Texas. She is thinking *Alamo, tabasco sauce, long neck beer.*
Even her thoughts of beer seem ominous.
The man is not clairvoyant, he can't read Fate's mind.
He is starting to get hungry and his left leg has gone to sleep.
He can't sleep because the trunk is too dark. He is bound,
so he can't stick his finger through the two-inch hole
that has been bored into the top of the brass trunk.
He doesn't know if it is day or night. Fate, on the other hand,
      is happy.
She is singing an old Everly Brothers song, *Dream, dream, dream, dream,*
when I want you all I have to do is dream. She is not thinking of a lover.
She is thinking *clean white sheets, a motel ashtray, the cool pink tile of a*
      borrowed bathroom.
To tell the truth, she is really thinking of her son.
She is happy because at this moment, speeding down the highway,
sliding over the hot baking asphalt, she is in control.

III. You Follow Fate and Man is Silent

In our last episode Fate, dressed like Jayne Mansfield,
was whizzing down the freeway with the man in tow, the man
      being bound
and gagged in a brass trunk, of course. We left you
at the ferris wheel, your cotton candy in the dirt,
mud on your new white dress. But that's not for you, no, not for long.
You hurry along to the little trailer you call home.
Beneath a needlepoint poodle you slip out of your dress,
as easy as a hand sliding out of a handcuff.
You step in the shower for one warm gust of water.

Then you powder your skin with talc and slip into something a little
        more comfortable,
a red satin camisole, a round flowered skirt.
If you stopped and twirled,
your skirt would rise around you. It might knock a ceramic penguin
off a shelf. But you don't twirl; you're in a hurry. You are determined
        to beat Fate
at her own game. You climb into a small red sportscar
and off you go, sailing down the highway. A small voice in your head
        says *Texas*,
so that is the way you go. In two days you are crossing the border.
You are heading toward El Paso. You stop for Mexican food
and a shot of tequila. For two days you have been thinking about
        your lover,
crammed into a brass trunk in the back of his mother's Cadillac.
You are starting to feel claustrophobic.
When a man at the Mexican restaurant asks you for the time
you start to cry. You wipe your face with the back of your hand—
your lover was once *this close* to you—and you hit the highway
        once again.
When you see the white Cadillac parked by the roadside you touch
your brakes, but not quickly enough. You skid into the Cadillac
and you all land in a ditch: Fate, your lover, and you, with a tiny
        trickle
of blood running down your chin. *Am I dying?* you ask yourself,
and you wonder *is this all?*

IV. Fate Shows Man His Destiny

Keeping in mind that Fate looks like Jayne Mansfield, and you,
your lover and Fate are sitting in a ditch outside El Paso,
let's continue with the story. Fate jumps out of her Cadillac
and throws open the trunk. Before you pass out you see the
        glistening brass
trunk inside the trunk of her car. It is this brass trunk
that has swallowed your lover whole, like Jonah.
You see marshmallow stars swimming above Texas, and then your
        eyes go black.

Meanwhile, Fate inquires after your lover's health, and when he
      replies in the affirmative,
she drops a few candy red hots through the two-inch hole
in the top of the brass trunk, and off they shoot down the highway.
They hop a plane to Hollywood (that's Hollywood, California,
if you haven't already guessed). The man is still bound and gagged
in the brass trunk, but he has heard the magic word *Hollywood*
and he is planning to find you and sail to Venice Beach or Malibu.
When they get to Hollywood, Fate takes the man in the trunk
to a hotel off Rodeo Drive. She finally opens the trunk,
but he is still bound and gagged. Before he can say, *oh, mother,*
Fate, it's you, she spanks him playfully and sticks a hypodermic needle
through his pants. Then he can be released from his binding
because he is completely under her control. (Notice it took drugs
and not a magic spell.) She binds him to sit in a chair and he obeys.
Obedient, she says, *he always was obedient, if nothing else.*
Then she takes her golden clippers out and shears his black curls.
She lovingly dresses him in a white silk suit.
They have a mai tai by the pool, and a piña colada for the road.
She drives up to the giant sign that says *HOLLYWOOD*, high on
      the hillside.
It is ready to storm. She bids him climb the sign,
and of course, he does, carrying a martini all the while.
He stands swaying on the letter *D* and then he falls.
At that moment the sky bursts and a staff of lightning pierces
      the ground.

V. Fate Drinks a Toast to Man's Demise

Having seen her son fall from the towering *HOLLYWOOD* sign,
Fate runs down the hillside like she is being chased by fiery demons.
She hops into her Cadillac and speeds towards town.
As quickly as she thinks *my son is dead, what have I done?*
she also realizes *he was my hobby, my little doll, now*
what will I do? But when she sees her platinum head
reflected in the window of a shop off Rodeo Drive, she forgets
about it for a while. She buys a mink coat and two sables
with a credit card she stole from an oil man back in Texas.

She wears one of the sables into the street and a green van
pulls up beside her. On the side of the van there is a mural
of cows standing in a cloud bank. A man leans out the window
and pours a bucket of red paint over her head.
Murderer, he says, and she thinks about it
and decides he may be right. (She is thinking now about the minks
and not her son.) She has a bubble bath at the hotel
and hires a cab driver to take her to San Francisco.
(Keep in mind that money is no object for Fate.)
As she leaves Los Angeles, she falls asleep.
In her dream, she is sitting in a seedy little bar
off Hollywood and Vine. She is dressed like Marlene Dietrich,
a fedora pulled over one eye. You walk in and point a gun
in her direction. For a second she thinks of the Black Dahlia,
dismembered in some back lot. She thinks about snuff films
and burned fingers. Then she raises her glass and toasts your lover.
He's dead, she says, her voice guttural and low.
But this is all a dream. She is still sleeping
in the back seat of a yellow cab, winding its way up the coast,
moving toward her own fate in San Francisco.

VI. Man Bests Fate and You Make a Choice

Having left you in a ditch in Texas and seen her son fall
to his death, Fate is riding in a taxicab, heading for San Francisco.
She wakes with a start. For one long swooning moment, Fate believes
she is in the movie *Vertigo,* whirring through the forests
of giant sequoias, climbing the dizzying streets.
The cab driver drops her off at a little inn
on the water front. She goes into the bar.
It is dimly lit. She pulls her pink feathered cape
around her shoulders, having given up fur for fowl.
She orders a pink lady and begins rubbing rouge
into her cheeks. In her compact, her face gleams metallically.
She realizes, startled, that in one day she has aged remarkably.
She no longer looks like Jayne Mansfield, or Kim Novak,
no movie goddess she. The silvery face in the compact
bobs eerily. She is becoming Norma Desmond, trapped

in her own life like a decaying movie queen.
She looks up into the Budweiser mirror above the bar
and she starts, for you are standing there, the man behind you.
He holds a gun in her side. *Mother, I think it's time,*
he says, and Fate starts. He tells her that when he fell
from the *HOLLYWOOD* sign, he was caught
in the net of an angel who was fishing for stars.
He rescued you from your bed of amnesia
in a small hospital outside of El Paso, then you flew off together to
        find her,
and found her here, aging terribly in the mirror of a bar in
        San Francisco.
The three of you march out into the lamp-lit
street, down through Chinatown, and further, out onto the Golden
        Gate Bridge.
Fate is practically racing beside you, she seems to grow lighter
each minute. You look up at the stars pushing down
like a bowl smothering the bay. If you held your breath
you could count each tiny point of light.
Then suddenly there is a sparkle of purple.
and Fate explodes off the bridge into the bay,
scattering into the water like an armful of fireworks.
The man wipes a tear from his cheek. (She was his mother, after all.)
You look out into the water, the lights of the city tossing
in the waves. For a moment you want to slide through
the rails like a rag doll and surface limply
beneath the bridge. Instead you hook your arm through his.
Tonight let's go dancing, you say.

CLOUDY AND ISAAC

1.

Dry brush displayed its ancient veins
white out of white core of white
the knife dreamed
sacrifice on a hill near Burbank
at the motel on a dry Fourth

from the eye layer on layer toward
the white core. White out of white
no air or sun, quickly the boy turns
his mouth opens.

Manzanita burns with neither smoke nor flame
in California the air becomes film, a taut core
and history shivers between Kadesh and Shur
a caught ram

A deer trapped in briar torn
soaked in flies phosphoresces

It's autumn and a fire slow with anger
trudges across the hill
where from resonant light a hand throws a man
against a child, sticks and dirty sheets
over the child's bruises, heroin, the acid smell
of a knife blade

> if a boy dies his uncles bury him
> then the men cut their hair
> and lesions and pus on their legs
> acknowledge their loss

2.

You did not stop your hand from love or fear
you did not withhold your son
You lied, you brought a ram and left a boy
on the hill a burnt offering I
couldn't stop your hand. Revealed myself,
your people descendents of animals from
Jehovahjireh, white out of white
from the mountain. I
cursed you back to the morning

As soon as a woman's contractions grow strong and close
she collects soft grass she doesn't wake her husband.
If she gets pregnant before her child
leaves her breast she buries the newborn alive.
It has no name. The !Kung love their babies
The heat ran into the foothills
and across the cleft mountain
the stones cooled 5000 years
remained unburied

3. The Death of Isaac Enrique Serota

All right where did it happen?
            The Croft Motel in Burbank on July 4, 1984
            early morning
Was it the hour when the stars sing out together? You say he was
    murdered
on the Fourth of July? On fireworks day?
            He was two years old and died
            of "massive bleeding"
Big deal it happens all the time every year voices from the earth
open like roses, then comes "massive bleeding"
            They sodomized him with the cardboard tube
            from a hanger. Are there any more questions?
How long were they at the motel? Was his mother there? Did she kill
    him?

Ruth Serota nicknamed Cloudy was roaming with
José Guzman lifting car stereos
But did she kill him?
Her boyfriend Eric Guzman, José's cousin, remained
in the room with the boy and the tv
How long at the motel?
Fifteen days
Of course you take a motel room steal stereos shoot heroin
torture a baby fuck a little and watch tv for fifteen days
Wrappers from Taco Bell in the room McDonalds styrofoam
a bent coat hanger
hypodermic needles and routine child abuse
Yes the dance of the child abusers
Judgment is heavy, the boy's name was Isaac Enrique Serota
and his bed was in the closet
The dry bugs of July, they were dying too
close-winged, but who killed him?
Mr. Lim manages the Croft Motel seventeen dollars a night
Forget it
A few toys were in the closet, a long black hair was tied
around Isaac's penis

4.

Ascertainment will make possible
a list of crimes, we can abandon the altar
where the child's bones remain charred,
the smell still drifts across valleys
deer bleeding look up

In the newlyweds' room pictures of fat babies
hung on the walls, on the bed a cake
on a tray and two oranges, the two chairs
close together. A pair of trousers covered them
one leg for each chair for bride and groom
united forever. In defiance of history

they believed loyalty would be rewarded by
deliverance. Their sins traveled lightly
because sin was individual like seed.
No iron they said went into the Temple
for iron becomes weapons.
Gold silver frustration sandalwood peacocks
the dead child's eyes open flames
apes ivory, and the forty year reign
of a pleasure loving king correlative
to austere fire

a burning stick like a needle, a knife like a plunger
kindled high in a drift of pale smoke
juice spurts on the tongue you lie down
The Temple falls, the bride's feet
must not touch the floor.

5. Eric Guzman

They tell me he's dead I didn't kill him,
why would I kill two year old a kid
I think he was three. They should ask her
his mother, what was she doing with him?
They try to boss you around, everybody
I don't even know her just a little
what she says about me I can't answer.
I meet her two three times at the most the most
I'm out of work too busy finding a job

my hands all cut up with dishes kitchens
you can't heal you sleep you wake up
there's dirt in the sky and you slip all the time
(your fingernails hurt and that's one day)
but I want to know who can accuse me.
You go crazy, you open a door
and there's a lot of toilets. I'm a man
I can get all the pussy I want, you go Saticoy

Pacoima they hang all over you they don't cost
nothing that kind of woman.
Anybody could look at me I need to wash my face,
there's no way I could do that
he was breathing in the closet I was watching tv

(There were worms coming out of my mouth
my tongue was infected, the heat
of my face dried the towel anyway
I begin to crawl around the room looking for quarters
can't find any, the garbage air
pours on me) and that whore and José
left me alone he wasn't my kid
it wasn't me, I bought him Ding Dongs
I bought him those little donuts,
we gave him some seeds he vomited
we gave him Tylenol
he couldn't shit you know
we was trying to help him
I'd say somebody else came in

we were having a good time, the fire in my face
I was dizzy my eyes sweat but what I saw
some kind of executioner came in the room
I'm just kidding the hot stones (the smoke
got hold of my cock) Jesus I've been so hungry
I need a doctor for my hands, my back
begins to twist so I can't sleep
I've been tricked too many times, people say
do this do that and I do it
that's my problem, I kicked out
my first wife I lived in Downey
she took the kid I never seen him
where he is I don't know Jackie, John
I'd say this executioner he was small
and he wore these little black gloves
the kid cried because he tripped against

the tv he had on these plastic diapers
he was constipated that's why we
the man hit him in the face believe it
or not you know I wasn't feeling so good
that skinny whore gone what a smell in that place
like burning shit it's not so funny
and that little guy hits the kid in the face
knocked him the fuck down screaming
like it was my fault. My cousin José
what could he tell you, nobody after him
he can tell you, but she and him was out

stealing you know stereos. What have I got.
I add it up a cheap watch three rings
a gold chain they're supposed to be keeping
my stuff up in Burbank
I don't know who sold the fucking stereos
I don't know, so many people have stole
me there's a lot of guys down here scoring
but I just want to clear my name.
(Sometimes the sound of the air there's nothing
to stop me I slip into my cock my feet
don't touch the ground) yesterday or day before
I sent away my wife my car broke, all you
can do is steal what stops me whispering
little hands in black gloves, that whore
with her mouth open her and all of them
lined up with perfume in the Silver Moon
pushing through to stop it all stop it

6.

The mountain went on writing, unreadable
but what it said might save us
our pain might save us

The trees would have dissolved
the silken ashes of the child
that settled on the hair of laborers bent
5000 years over a small grave

The animal swayed carrying broken-tongued sticks
through the land of Moriah
the thoughtless bark like wrapped fists
Abraham reading signs of himself
moving slowly. He could see
a hut and smoke on the far hill
a low wall under torn grey
turning small figures
toward almost no one

And he walked alone with his dead son
the dead generations
snared by sight

7.

        Blood in blue webs rose
        in the transparent bloom of his skin, Isaac sat
        in a burning chair his head turned
        this fire had no inner name

Let me tell you the kids were in the room
crying three to seven years old
they knew something was going to happen
to their wee-wees, when they saw the barber
and the straight razor they threw up

and they fouled themselves this was serious.
Older brothers uncles and fathers held them
they were slippery as water the men laughed
like trees hiss and clack branches,

and over a hole dug in the floor they lifted
a boy legs tugged apart. The barber grabbed
a penis pulled the foreskin swiped it
screams, men grinned clenching teeth remembering themselves

Into the hole dropped foreskins with blood
the men brought cornstalks cut in triangles
pouches for maimed little ones
then the boys ate chicken stew with hot spice
cold chicken soup with hot spice but no lemon
which could make them impotent. Relatives
with food or toys made of cornstalks arrived,
with toy flutes music of cornstalks, the boys' wee-wees
tied against their bellies

When the boys healed their uncles bathed them
the barber shaved their heads they put on shorts
and white shirts, couldn't be naked
the barber earned his hot meal and roast chicken
while the poor ate cakes of black-eyed peas paste
cakes of millet cakes of wheat

8.

The brown hands of Sarah
mother Magdalena and daughter Cloudy
helpless in Burbank stone

Eric Guzman's fist raised
the stippled arm raised
            José start praying the baby
            stopped breathing, Cloudy start praying
            "It was a regular prayer" Cloudy says
            wondering "like Jesus help this baby
            Your blood is the holy something"
            shimmering on a folded blanket

9. Abraham

My eyes feel the sour wind
music wakes in Sarah's lashes
will they say I killed him because of her?
to save my life?
my arm trembles with memory
it fell as if a rope had broken
and he died, I didn't know that anger dragged me
up the hill, or left a ram there sizzling jointed
for my lord's small appetite
no neither there nor here but in me
stretched along a road

Or did he come back down with me
trailing by my hand, Isaac
skipping off the memory so he could
inherit me, our circumcized company
the future earned
so I could say now Sarah here's your son
you were beautiful once fight for him
we're blessed by death
remember the smell of the fat cities burning
it's the same, ask the weeds ask spiders
       O Isaac your milky cheek
       the smell of your mouth
       I've broken the water's soft bones
       the sand my people
Everyone I killed was myself everyone
I spared myself I've done little
my children will feed the season's
black burnt wood to God
until ashes and wisps of curls
fill twilight

and I'll say that I was here
tangled in the hills

that my will served the future
the way the hovering birds back there
serve the air as faint heat
rising brushes them

10.

       Eric back from Costa Rica
       phones Magdalena, "You'll die
       Magdalena for what you said about me"

Isaac grew old, eyelashes white
he couldn't see his sons
the smell of skin and hair Esau's
       but put the body in the *makara*
       we don't need a lid, cover it
       with the white cloth
       the broken pot thrown in the grave
       reminds us, but the names
arrange the names on the mountain
Milcah and Nahor, Cloudy and Eric,
Kemuel, Chesed and Pildash, Magdalena
Jackie, the judge, and Martha Potera
to remind us that Eric took the stereos
when he ran away

       To remind us
"At the time," the detective said, "I didn't
have enough to suspect full-blown abuse.
All I know was what the grandmother told me"
Sitting in the lime green house in the rocker
near the swamp cooler Magdalena said
you should have seen the beautiful party

for his first birthday
Not enough to suspect full-blown abuse

no one asks Abraham no one asks about the firewood
no one suspects full-blown abuse

To the nurse in Mission Hills Cloudy said
Isaac caught his head in a metal gate
No one at the Cotte d'Arms two doors
from the Croft Motel on the Fourth of July
suspects full-blown abuse by Cloudy
going out midnight to steal stereos
the baby breathing in the closet
across from the Arco station

"It's a lot of Monday morning quarterbacking"
the detective said, "I told her
don't let that baby out of your sight."
At Magdalena's house
"No se puede pasar par aqui" five dusty cars
settle under fronds in the driveway
"A lot of second-guessing is involved
you take a look back at a case like this"
where it says "Coin Laundry Open 6-to-9"
And the Lord visited Cloudy as he had said
near Church's Fried Chicken and the Lord
did unto Cloudy as he had spoken
and then ran away, the burns on Isaac's
hands and lips Cloudy said were accidents

"She loved the baby"
plea bargaining in Pasadena for voluntary
baby slaughter below scarred Burbank hills
she was "Cloudy" in the Latin Life gang
tattooed at 13 the runaway
that Eric jammed the cardboard hanger tube
into Isaac, the punishment in the closet
his nest on San Fernando Road

"It is only the esthetic writer who thinks lightmindedly
that he extols the power of love by letting the lost man
be loved by an innocent girl" Eric and Cloudy
together in the Croft Motel with the color tv by RCA
plea bargaining with the sky before morning

11.

The kinds of offering are the peace-offering
the burnt-offering the covenant sacrifice
and the libation, then in the motel

we find the sodomizing-offering and the beating
unto death with the fist
the hair tied around the penis offering
hardly controllable in Burbank at the curve
of San Fernando Road across from the post office
was the holocaust which is the burnt-offering
of the whole animal ask the clerk at Roy's

Junior Market, Isaac a sacred animal
a camel without flaw bound on an altar
of piled stone, not to hack off flesh
his small body with swords alone in the room
with the RCA to give the baby
as a gift large and small cattle sheep and lambs
goats and kids the wild pigeon as well
and the blood and fat very appropriate
to invite the stones as guests
and which part of Isaac goes to Cloudy
and which to Eric which to Magdalena
who cries in her rocker looking at the picture
and which to Jackie the social worker, the holy community,
the reporter the judge each gets a part
that the sky might be well-disposed and earthquakes
you couldn't boil Isaac in Cloudy's milk
because she didn't have milk it had drained

out through the needle, if you catch Eric
you can say why did you do this
the argument for human sacrifice
depends on Zebah and Zalmunna killed
by Gideon and Agog by Samuel

The searing of the dove's wing
an agreement in stone
the blood on the dry pavement
the blood of both smeared on stone
dividing the carcass
cutting oxen in pieces
Hey man Cloudy's a bitch man
what you want the kid for
reminds you she's a whore
got to have some fun
going to Pacoima find José
carnitas with shit from Costa Rica

Pull out the afterbirth and burn it
wean the baby with wild heliotrope
on the mother's nipples
Abraham who can't understand
who he spared from the altar
his jaw and fear

12.

Darkness elongates the drug
into sharp turns the side streets
Ruth and José hook an Alpine a Kenwood
two Pioneers, they're gone
fast across Burbank North Hollywood
the roads are clear Magnolia Boulevard
summer mist cocoons the lights
to get away clean
screwdriver and prybar beneath the seat

20 second instruments devices
perform eviscerations, offerings to the poor
resulting from small acts of craft
learned quickly in delight
they rip-off stereos in the dark morning
in thickets, quiet neighborhoods

> Cloudy won't skate the kitchen
> making garbage but fly streets
> for Eric Guzman, does he
> inflict death on a living creature
> not by blood infusion but by fist?

This small boy can be used for pleasure
he drinks milk and laughs like his mother
in a gurgle his long face of Magdalena
in the photo with roses

nothing lost because despair keeps nothing
for itself he's gravel beneath the mesh gate
"No se puede" near the leaf blanket
the proper work of two-petaled new grass

as Cloudy and Eric sink into him
and there lifted by Magdalena there
held in her smokey kiss shuddering
against her breast they gaze
through his unmoving eyes at great fronds

13.

Section 187 with malice aforethought murder
Isaac Enrique Serota a human being
Section 273 (a) (1) between 7/4/83 and 7/4/84
under circumstances likely to produce bodily harm
and death, injure cause and permit a child
Isaac Enrique Serota to suffer and to be inflicted

with unjustifiable pain and mental suffering
and having care and custody of said child
injure cause and permit the person and health
of said child to be injured and did willfully
cause and permit said child to be placed in such
a situation that his person and health was endangered
Section 289 penetration of genital and anal
openings of Isaac Enrique Serota by a foreign
object substance instrument and device to wit
a coat hanger tube against the will of said victim
and by force violence duress menace and fear
of unlawful bodily injury to said victim
and to another for the purpose of sexual arousal
gratification and abuse

14.

So summing up we define sacrifice
as an act belonging to worship

in which a material oblation
such as Isaac Enrique Serota
two years old is presented to deity
and consumed in his service
and which has as its goal
through communion economic favor and pleasure
that is to say of necessity

Evidence of universal favor glows
from tv and lamp
in Room 11 of the Croft Motel
managed by Robert Lim, scene of a former murder
the brown drape lined with plastic
the great cape the mirror of contrition
and labor, the dresser the swag lamp
and the RCA color tv on a swivel

where Eric and Cloudy and José shoot heroin
quickly and that which ascends
is the burnt offering never ending
"the firstborn of thy sons shalt thou give
unto me" and the libation was of blood
and tearing around the anus
the animal must be without blemish
in the marrow of the soft universe
wherein the ritual includes the imposition of hands
slaughter of the victim at the door
of the tabernacle, because catastrophe rises
flaying and cutting up the carcass
washing the entrails and legs
sprinkling the blood about the altar
where it stiffens

Dispose the pieces on the wood of the altar
burn the offering
among the green fronds, huge green feathers
ragged and shining over Magdalena's house
into flat white sky

15.

He walked down the slope tired
soon he would bury Sarah
the sweat had chilled his forehead
as he watched a brush of smoke
in the valley, he wasn't hungry
behind him at a distance followed
his two servants and the ass
not laden moving easily
and further back the weapon
on the smouldering altar darkened

and the mouth of the ground closed
he stumbled and drove his stick hard

into the ground slowing down
and remembering saw nothing stayed his hand
had no will
while wires and neon paused
they would say where is your son
he would say nothing
as if he couldn't understand
the twigs stiff and powdered by drought
though he knew Abimilech would be drinking
in his tent and others in the camp
holding children, the future
poured ahead of him toward home
he desired the inevitable

which is Cloudy pulling thin fingers
through her hair and staring at her hand
there with lint Lysol and six years
in Frontera already credited 704 days
she waits to be released and maybe Eric again

CHILD BRIDE

Our first night together we slept with it
between us, thick as your arm. You showed me
what was yours and what was mine: a comb,
mirror, pitcher for water and somewhere small
to put my doll. When you looked at me I knew
you waited for the 'day of the flood' and you asked
when my sisters became *mahi*. This I did not know
and told you that. When you believed nothing
I said, you took a reed and whipped me. There,
I thought, there's blood. You said "If you love me
you will kiss it on the lips." When I ran away
my father took me back to you and you forgave
his debt. My straw doll tells me not to worry,
the spirits watch over us. It is worst at night
with the sound of wind in the trees and I feel
a wetness there, between the legs.

LUNCHEONETTE, LIVE OAK, FLORIDA

A lard moon wanes on the griddle.
Tobacco sweetens in tins. Two men
recommend the chili, ask where I'm from.
I want to answer *here*, where drawls
thicken the air like jasmine and gold teeth
sharpen on sunlight. I want to save their voices
in books, their talk of shoats and sorghum
inviting as poured coffee.

My shoes slipped off, I lean across the counter
striking up words like matches, wondering
what it's like when they take off their
flannel shirts. Outside I follow
their thick arms pointing to the highway.
By the time I reach the next state
I realize the place reads well
just once, like a short story.

MY TRUE HAND

in my dream my left hand
was my true hand
before I was slapped down
& learned to tell lies
use my right to reach
for food & money
& pull the blanket over my head at night

□ Myra Sklarew □

EXCHANGE
For Eleutheria and Koula

In the morning
the children tease me
giving me the word *melon*
for *shoe. Carpousi,*
they laugh, pointing
to my foot. I imagine
a great ripe cantaloupe.

In the evening
they take both
my hands and pull me
into the sky.
Tell us, they whisper
in Greek, what you call that,
they say, pointing
to a firmament so alive
with stars you cannot see
the dark places.
And tell us, they say,
pointing to the slice of moon,
golden as the cheese ripening
on the stone porches
under silken mulberry trees,
what it is named.

And I think to tell them
straight away, opening
my language to them
like a gift brightly wrapped,
though it is fair to say here
I was tempted to teach them

eyebrow in place of *star, button*
for *moon, scribble* for *sky,*
but I was leaving and I wouldn't
see them again,

so I unwrapped the words
and took them and opened their hands
and placed the words inside
so they could feel them
the way children in my country feel
the quivering body of a lightning bug
after it is caught, going off and on
that way in the warm small cave
of the palm.

□ *R. T. Smith* □

No Masks

on Ossabaw Island

I have ridden so long
down palmetto-flanked roads
that the cycle begins to become me,
a new kind of centaur
under long Spanish moss
and the shade of ancient magnolias.

Past the tabby houses
and their sharp walls of shells—
once slave quarters but lasting—
past the pasture where a new foal
sleeps in the sun.
I have entered the pine barrens
and found a dead end where garbage
is strewn on the ground, rusted
metal, cartons and carcasses
of beasts found dead or slain
that the guests may feast.

Perhaps I have eaten meat
from the cow whose head is all
of her that survived, horns
pointing to a black crown
of buzzards above, one eye
catching me to the quick.

Perhaps I have dreamed
of the boars and sows whose bones
and rags of rank fur
haunt this end of the road.
Two black feral pigs dart
in green underbrush; the shadows

of a dozen buzzards descend
and mercifully rise.
Do the wild burros come here
to browse? Does the island's sole
white Brahma bull stray here?
Only the scavengers are attracted
to the outlines of lost life,
the lessons of broken skulls
and the jawbone biting ash.

Herons in near wiregrass call,
and the sun comes from behind a cloud.
This is the road that folds
back on itself, the one-way path
I can choose to retake.
On the bicycle again, wheels
spinning bright spokes to the sun,
I feel my weight on each pedal,
lean for home, try to remember
not to come back to this crater
where dead fate wears no masks,
try to believe both the hunted
beasts and scavengers are all
acceptably Other, try to keep my eye
on the flight of a beautiful heron.

□ *Andrew Sofer* □

THE ANATOMY OF WHALES

The hornlike strips inside the upper jaw
are used for corset stays. Wax ambergris
culled from intestine makes perfume fixative,
and spermaceti candles, ointments, musk
boil down from fatty acids in the head
whose bones are carved in delicate scrimshaw.

The arctic narwhal is hunted for its tusk:
Old Norsemen named it corpse-whale, *narhvalr,*
because ice-pallid skin glowed like sunken flesh.
In Greenland, seals are frighted from the water
by sculling kayaks shaped like killer whales.
The Inuit then club the seals to death.

They say that dolphins call in dialects,
study in schools and mourn the loss of friends,
while pods of orcas have returned small pets
washed overboard to shore, and have been seen
holding funerals for a dead leviathan:
buoying the body, singing to the drowned.

Tonight, I dream whales plying through black ocean:
grief sounding through them like a radio
insistent in its threnody of moon,
joining the kelpies' chorus of the wake
only to let the dead weight fall below,
each note a wasted spiracle of breath.

WAR

My mother said he was real,
not a friend but my father, home,
finished with a war as he snapped
rubber bands around each lobster's
red claws in that Boston apartment.
Helplessness was what he had
even before the salt poured
its shadowy stream into the kettle,
his lobsters wobbling an altered race
across the linoleum as he winked
and took my mother by the hand,

took me to the bedroom with the fold-away
cot. I sucked my thumb, stroked her satin slip
I kept for the dark, wishing it was dark.
He stood behind her with his big gold
bourbon glass, his breath moving
in her hair. Out of her hair,
as he came closer and pulled the slip
from my hand, pulled my thumb from my mouth,
all of Boston's winter rushing the opened window.

He flung the satin slip. In a flutter
it dimmed like a child's ghost
with all that darkness beneath. I saw
the moves of a soldier, his hands
finishing at the window,
seven floors up in the dark.

AMERICAN SPEECH

*"Some argue that Gibbs has yet to be fully understood nearly ninety years after his
death. With his findings in thermodynamics, and the subsidiary fields of statistical
mechanics and vector analysis, however, he singlehandedly laid the foundations for
vast portions of modern science, and is now widely regarded as the greatest scientist
ever to work at Yale, and the foremost American scientist of all times."*

—Marc Wortman, "A Loner's Legacy," 1989

1

Resistance to tyrants *is* obedience to God.
        Don't Tread On Me!
            The Connecticut Valley

has to be
        the most
                abstract location in the universe—minds

of winter, minds of Iceland spar, at work
        in Dickinson, Edwards,
                Peirce,

and Gibbs. The whole a hotbed
        of revival, of Great Awakening: the one
                word

Noah Webster invented, of all those
        in his book,
                demoralise,

a slow
        seep into melting snow and gray afternoon;
                Gibby, skating

long strokes on the pond; Emily
        watching freedom
                condense

inside the clear glass of her window.
    In this Valley, neighbors
        disregard

—sustain—hidden fervence, run Underground
    railroads; *Images and Shadows*
        sewn up

in Edwards's notebooks, flint
    stitched into Dickinson's, 700
        equations

of Gibbs's great paper set up in type at last
    by shopkeepers'
        subscription: in CT, they

Make Do, but they tore
    the house, the home on High Street, Gibbs's—born
        and died there—down.

    2 "It Is You Talking Just as Much

as myself—I act as the tongue
    of you," he said, or wrote: Walt Whitman. *Who?* Who *is*
        this massing, polled, this multi-point self?

"I showed her Heights she never saw—
    And now— 'Woulds't have me for a Guest?'
        She could not find her Yes—"

Dickinson wrote. Then
    re-wrote, *as*
        "He showed me heights I never saw—"

Deeper
    duplicity: none. Role, trope, and object: all
        reversing, as if all were one

affair—
>of language.
>>Cooing,

the bird outside my window takes no notice,
>mid-morning or dawn or supper, it is mournful: *Oh but—who-who-who* the form of its floating

sorrow, so intent
>and equable now in its sorrow, so patient
>>and outbreathing

now, of its sorrow. I had
>hoped to find the iris tended,
>>still, in Gibbs's garden; I thought women

of that town, if they had
>a garden club, or League, would come with dark blue
>>bulbs

or yellow-tongued; I thought they would keep
>a Garden, but
>>they tore it

limb from limb, beheading, dripping, tore the house
>on High
>>Street down.

>3 Emily Elizabeth Dickinson, 1830-1886
>Josiah Willard Gibbs, 1839-1903

Never married, never moved from their Family Home.

>*I am so potent, I can reach you only after wave upon wave*
>*of dilution. You will re-discover, but not read me.*
>*I have built a language to make my work more pure.*

A pure inquiry—into unity—has concerned this nation
ever since it claimed Independence through union. Cornerstones
of the Church on the Green in New Haven, monuments

to Regicide: Dickinson, a Fire Bride, a bomb, a volcano. As alive,
or more so, in the grave as out of it. Showing us this across the garden
fence of the grave. Speaking in the tomb, of the tomb, as of a ride,

one of many, every poem one of many, No-name inquiries—
but we have her numbered. *Is* Dickinson articulate? Did Higginson,
Johnson, Franklin—would Bloom, if Bloom spoke of her—make her

articulate? She said the grave gave her language.
Whitman said the future, always sampling the future, enlisting the future,
and Gibbs a prisoner, of his own unwillingness to auction

his mind, who built a mathematic language to make his work *more pure*—
who made it so pure, it sublimed instantly into zones of power
and remains enthroned there, isolated there. The supremely

articulate among us, *Amistad* Africans, mutineers for freedom
on the ship they commandeered, stole from the captain and steered
by their own light—and by starlight—to a New World, a rock-bound

coast; a world not wilderness alone, but Wilderness with courts
in it, and canon, and codes of presentation, a world of sacred
language their own language attacked, active virus, ancient

knowledge that it was, *they* perplex—No translator.
No way-maker. No wizard wise woman sponsor. Only the Valley
itself of the Connecticut River, who brought from itself,

with the help of Sarah, Jonathan Edwards. A valley
itself with its snow and snow water. So far from Home.

> *I am so potent, I can reach you only by submitting*
> *to wave upon wave of dilution. So potent*
> *only I can reach you: now. Soon.*

4

So
to frame observation
as to make God speak: science creates

alert, disciplined—regenerate—perception. Absolute
validity
of the sensuous

>   in CT: *We could never have conceived of these,*
>   *if we had not seen them; and now, we can think of nothing*
>   *beyond them,*

Edwards said. The obliquity
of love does not in fact disable it. Frank celebration
being

>   denied, direct apprehension: the Truth set out
>   before him, naked, leaning through a veil
>   of shifting snow, awaits

elucidation. Have we moved no
farther, then—than
from ingenuity to insight, private judgment with a vengeance?

Men hate
to die, Edwards said, *because they cannot bear*
to let go of the beauty of the world,

>   but Dickinson
>   said,
>   *I guard My Master's Head —*

5

Gibbs making found

what lies hidden, so deeply nested
is it within, so down
deeply pocketed, miles

from the icy, calm, notational
surface: making a line,
a lure, one symbol, one elliptical

expression, holding echo
upon echo, decoding
to a catalog: an infinite

acceptance . . .

detonation

as almost welcome and always
implicit
in the mind, like the cloud, low,
and going to snow

in CT. Great still pool. Demoralized
desire that waits for
snow
as if the snow were

winged

INSIDE THE WOLF

—*"The good grandmother . . . cried, 'Pull the bobbin, and the latch will come up!'"*

Red Ridinghood is puzzled:
I am so far into this odd death

with my convalescent reek and flannels,
lemon and green-apple glycerine,

my old woman's whiskery breath.
I ride the forest

close to the floor. The engines
of the beast's digestion

roll and toil; it is
how we used to feel the autumn

coming on, a sudden spill
of cold that ruins bittersweet,

the chicory still holding,
blind stars in frost. A rind

of dream, I lie inside
the great belly's curve, the head

that goes before me blurs
and smears, galactic, cold. A hole

that forms the eye is torn
into the zodiac; this is the gap

through which I steer. A thread
of sourness follows me

the way it does the very old.
I know that I was not

delicious! No, the child
will not regret me, nor the stamens

torn from scarlet betony
in fall, the seeds unlatched.

LETTER FROM MALAYSIA

I have arranged a marriage, my mother wrote,
for your sister and the third son
of the Tong family. He is single,
and he died ten years ago. Your sister
liked him at the viewing ceremony,
the medium said, and promises to behave
once she is wed. It has been a terrible time
since your brother's wedding. Sickness
in the house, his bride screamed every night
in her sleep, their dreams troubled by hands
squeezing their throats.

Secretly I went to the temple,
begged Kuan Yin's help. The medium said:
it was your sister, eighteen years quiet
in her grave, roused by her brother's marriage,
desires her own.

You know your brother: he laughs at me
and my faith. He knows nothing about this.
I tell you because she would like you
to know and rejoice at her happiness,
you were so close in her life.

   One other thing, your brother's wife
has stopped screaming in her sleep since
the marriage was announced to the ancestors.

Thank the goddess everyone is healthy now.

GOOD NEWS

You finally got out of that silent blue room.

For most of October I remembered to hope
that someone would take you outside to watch
trees strip down in thudding reds
and one orange pulse (though there aren't many trees
where the edge of Boston's brick meets Roxbury,
where you looked out on one scratch pine, your eyes going,
all season, waiting for November to stop).

When your brother the minister called me, he said
"It's good news"; he was manic, probably crazy
with relief that the year is almost over,
and I was predictable, I spoke softly,
I used the word *arrangements.* But I saw

them taking you out under tan and black trees,
all the color ground into compost now.
How can I believe that you've "gone home"?
Did you peel away your body, blighted sapling
that imprisoned you in a cloven pine
and emerge as my hostaged memory of you—
a red-haired man dancing to high-life music,
a man who drowned rats in a bucket in Zaire
writing to his mother *I'm trying not to hurt you?*

The poems I wrote about you are carbon
and guides for the tongue. They are not one friend
squeezing the pulp of another for copy.
They are not your private Elysian Fields.

I don't have your brother's ringside seat
on heaven. I can believe in this:
the shade of your hair on Skyline Drive

(a rust I can barely pick out from the trees),
what you wrote: "Life is short and I love him,"
that you knew who I was three weeks before you died,
and that your mother, who gagged when you told her
you touch men, was there feeding you by hand.

MUD DOG

My child sings a song about mud.
Mud on my knees. Mud on my clothes.
Mud house. Mud mother. Mud dog.
Dog in the mud. The dog in the mud
she wants to draw. She has dreamed
of the dog. Now she remembers.
And we must search the house for the dog.
Her brother says, It's in your head,
and that for a moment stops her.
She loves herself so much

she wants to put her head in all our laps
and let us hold it for a while.
She wants to put both legs in the same
opening of her underpants.
She wants me to buy her a dog. I say
the sound of my heart
makes dogs bark.
And she smiles and pretends to hear a dog
the red bark of the dog,
the red eyes of the dog rising,
black fur and enormous, the dog that has learned
to stand on two legs now. He's coming

to eat his fill, to fill
his stomach of crumbling mud.
He's coming even in dreams. He's coming
even in the child-smell of her hair,
in the dirty water
of the bath after mud,
even in the smell of soap.
Even for her.
Even for my child.

SIDESTEP

at the Folger Shakespeare Library Guest House

Always there will be
people in the courtyard
whose voices gesticulate like hands,
urging a question to its end.
And the radio next door
beating on the wall
like an hysterical child.
Why do they berate themselves
with loud, insistent voices?
Why don't they turn,
and step out of their lives—
as certain women step out of skirts
and turn to their lovers with smiles.

Playing with Fire

I caution you, my father said,
never play with fire. I have

played with fire ever since.
I have seen sunsets in South Vietnam

to make Hawaii bleak.
Others mistook them for 'palm,

they were that bright
and bloody red. They made

the concertina wire
looking like branding iron.

The Montagnards in Montreal
still hunt for food in the heart

of the city. Bow and arrow,
bare hands, knives. They hunt

for squirrels, dogs and cats,
anything loose. I have seen

their charred faces,
the point of fire in their eyes.

The boat people come to Philadelphia
by way of Malaysia, Texas, Ohio and Delaware.

They change their names
to bypass the quotas. They say

they come from Malaga,
Penang, Guam, Kuala Lumpur,

but I know they are Vietnamese
by the heat in their eyes,

the betel nut stains on lips and gums,
the smell of dead cabbage on their breath,

the way they wear white shirts to class
like uniforms. The shrill voice,

the nervous laugh, the bow-legged
walk on spider's legs, all

of these things give them away.
He said his name was Armistice Singsong,

come from Malaysia to take my class—
College Comp. 50.

He sat near the wall, looked out
the window, listened for noises.

He stared at me when called upon,
as though I had insulted him,

broken his ancestors' bones in some way.
He wrote themes on torture,

hunger, helplessness.
By mid-semester he had dropped out

without an official withdrawal.
The snow melted and he was gone.

The Buddhist monks who burned themselves
are gone. I saw one once

near the tailor shops on Tudo Street.
A little, bald, bespectacled man.

His orange robe and beggar bowl
were color-coupled with the flames.

I saw the glasses melt on his face
and wondered that he kept them on.

I burned my draft card during Tet
from a chopper over Cam Ranh Bay.

Who knew? I was already there,
so nobody cared. Women back

in the world burned bras.
That drew a crowd.

In the panoply of impulse disorders,
arson is a male disease.

And I think to myself
in late summer's heat

when six western states
have forest fires raging out of control

that these are vets of Vietnam
speaking to each other

the way the Indians used to do
before they became extinct.

Teaching the Dark

for my night class in writing

Tonight there'll be bridges down
all along my way, and small soft things
charging my headlights: not moths.
The signs will be changed, and point
impossible routes: cut-off sky
or the ground. By the roadside, branches
will scoop their difficult lessons
across my gaze: bad curves, iced slopes,
the fear of sleep.
    If the radio sucks in
strange stations, a voice will whisper
how to hunt deer with a bent pulphook;
during the weather, it will darken
as though asking beneath words: *Help me—*
I'm yours.
    I will go on
somehow, hoping the steel ton under me
knows home. Remembering men
returned from old wars, by night
and with all kin maybe lost, in stories
I would never tell you to dream.

□ *Ronald Wallace* □

AT THE VIETNAMESE RESTAURANT

Her father plops his ice cream on his place mat
and scoops his sticky rice into his lap,
then shoves his fortune cookie at his wife,
insists it's hers. What should her mother do?
Spoonfeed him? Be embarrassed? Or pretend
that nothing's wrong? What happened to the man
she's known for fifty years? Where has he gone?
He checks his watch as if he can still read it.

It's late. It's late. It's much too late, he thinks.
*And here he is lost in this foreign country
with strangers at the table. His heart sinks.
How will he get home? Where might that be?
He'll smile and do his best to be polite,
although he's seated with the enemy.*

IMPERATIVES

Listen. I am a skin
of old voices. Childhood
scrambled out of my arms before
I knew it and no wonder.
Consider the eye, a small form
of blindness. Consider
the grasping hand. Touch salt
to your lips and remember
oceans and grief, the
crystal nights of all too many
centuries, jihad's red teeth.
Touch flesh and old murder,
the poisoned wells of longing,
stones of anger worn
to small precious gems
too expensive to part with.
Bathe, but the body never comes
clean. You carry dust
in your clothes. Gum black bread
in the tents of despair. Go. Throw
death's cape over your shoulders.
Walk into the frozen night,
your breath ghosting away before
you. I tell you such snow
is cold innocence.
Refuse to worship the moon. Plow
the ancient fields of mourning.
Plant corn's gold tooth.
Learn the patience
of sunlight, the extra-
ordinary compassion
of rain.

□ *Nancy G. Westerfield* □

ON RAILROAD STREET

Taking the train East, and its first
Sidle away from the station paralleled
Railroad Street, with the Farmers Bank,
Rexall Drugs, and Tex's Corner Cafe;
Then the increasing amble passed the ends
Of avenues stubbed with signs: Plum and Railroad,
Pleasant and Railroad, Locust and Railroad,
Until the quickening click of the wheels
Swung a wide arc south of town, and the frail
Steeple of Countryside Christian lost the street-
Grid in the fields.

            Taking the train West
Away from the twisted riddle of city people,
And the easy travel of the final mile
Parallels Railroad Street, picking it up
At Spotts Garage, Henry's Idle Hour,
And the Everlasting Brick Corporation,
Where the kilns keep their huddle
Like primeval barrows. Locust and Railroad,
Pleasant and Railroad, Plum and Railroad,
And the slackening click of the wheels
Looks beneath elms to the station lawn;
Railroad Street drifts the scent of roses
And a hint of brakeshoes; evening's train is gone.

NAPOLEON'S SNUFFBOX

A tight blue suit fits
too well on you, buttons and boots
snapped up, glossy,

cordon sprinting the short chest
where your heart was
before you plucked it out.

The snuffbox contains your portrait,
a rim of rubies,
pigeon's blood, bright as a bullet.

It pumps and sniffs itself
but does not sneeze. Open it.
Lift back the cool lid like an eye.

Look, a little mirror hangs
over perfumed dust. You could bring it close
if you marry it, give it children.

But you can't, you pinch
a rub of powder between softness and whiteness,
stubby finger, the opposing thumb.

You singe the mother of Russia
with your breath
but the city is empty.

You have it and have it! your victory
over love, punchglass full.
Moscow burns but it's only wood.

Only a scent and not the present taste.
Snuff stains your teeth
but not the lid's miniature.

Body parts stuck to snow
snicker at your feminine secrets.
Runt of the chosen

with fat, pale hands, one punctures
the vest, chilled,
searching out ribs

where a hole dries, pinched and emptied.
O father
of every country, I know you

are starving
the men. The road looks back at you,
a dust of glass.

Gangrene won't stink when limbs
freeze, *horoshow, c'est ca.*
You taste only what gods taste,

salt honey
of their own fresh blood,
addictive tedium of dust.

You sniff, the whole murderous sky
bayonets one throat.
You and you.

FRITZ, THE ADJUSTER

We told the pregnant girl she would have to get out,
Though her husband was gone and she had no place to go.
The company wanted its trailer back. She had missed
Too many payments. We helped her pack and sent her
Off in tears. Then we drank the sixpack that someone
Had left in the ice box.
                            Years ago, the first time
I drank a can of beer, a mouse ran up my arm
And lodged himself in the hole between my eyes.
Since then I cannot roust him out, though I have
Tempted him with peanuts, pickled eggs and Slim Jims
Until he paced and shrieked from his desperate hunger.

He makes me think; sometimes more than I'd like:
I wonder what Wanda would look like pregnant,
Wonder where she is, if she has money?

Some days you can be proud of what you do,
You want to tell the world how excellent you are,
How everyone should love you for just being you.
But today I think I'll smoke that mouse out
For good, put some sharp cheese on the trap,
Have one more beer when the bar goes *crack!*

SONG OF MYSELF

Eyes sprayed with shadows
I refuse to leave the house.
My skirts flare
in slow epiphanies of fire.

First break of cold.
Charm is a slipper, a flannel robe.
I stir secrets, crossing myself
for a poem, a new dress,
wanting to go.
                    Nothing can stop me.
Not even the sacred texts, my calendar
of repentance.
Dashing all those quiet hours
in one slide down the bannister,
one opening line, unbuttoning.

I enter my new self effortlessly.
Come quickly I call
and by the time you reach me
it is gone. Only after
                    calling it Spring
I suffer.

        Kiss me, make my skin light
and free! Am I pretty? Can I sing?
Ah, the language of desire,
how I perfect it, making a virtue

of divisions,
racing with myself to fall
at the first roadblock, to be loved.

CONTRIBUTOR NOTES

Henry Allen writes about American culture for *The Washington Post* and has published articles recently in *Vanity Fair, Forbes,* and the *New York Review of Books.* Houghton Mifflin published *Fool's Mercy* and Smithsonian Books a recent collection of essays, *Going Too Far Enough: American Culture at Century's End.* Dryad Press will bring out a chapbook early in 1997, *Glare and Other Poems.*

Paul Allen directs the Charleston Writers' Conference at the College of Charleston in Charleston, South Carolina.

Yehuda Amichai, one of the leading literary figures in Israel, lives in Jerusalem. Since 1955 he has published eleven collections of poetry in Hebrew, two novels, and a book of short stories. His work has been translated into thirty-three languages.

Susan Astor's poetry has been published in more than 100 magazines and anthologies. Her collection, *Dame,* was published by The University of Georgia Press in 1980. She works full time as a poet-in-residence in the public schools.

Mark H. Baechtel is a poet, fiction writer and freelance journalist. He has published stories and poems nationally in magazines and newspapers, and is curently on fellowship at the University of Iowa's Writer's Workshop.

John Balaban's *New & Selected Poems* will appear in 1997 from Copper Canyon Press. His earlier collections include *After Our War* (winner of the Lamont Award) and *Words for My Daughter,* a National Poetry Series selection. Balaban is also a novelist (*Coming Down Again*) and a memoirist (*Remembering Heaven's Face*).

Chana Bloch has published two books of poems, *The Secrets of the Tribe* and *The Past Keeps Changing*; a critical study, *Spelling the Word: George Herbert and the Bible*; and translations of the Biblical *Song of Songs* as well as the Israeli poets Dahlia Ravikovitch and Yehuda Amichai. She is Professor of English and Director of the Creative Writing Program at Mills College.

Michelle Boisseau's second volume of poems, *Understory,* was chosen by Molly Peacock as winner of the 1996 Samuel French Morse Prize and will be published by Northeastern University Press in November 1996. Her first book, *No Private Life,* was published by Vanderbilt University Press in 1995; with Robert Wallace she is author of *Writing Poems, 4th edition* (Harper Collins, 1995). She received a fellowship from the National Endowment for the Arts in 1989. Her poems have appeared in *The Gettysburg Review, The Southern Review, Agni, Ploughshares, The Ohio Review,* and many other journals.

Cathy Smith Bowers was a winner of the General Electric Award for Younger Writers, and received the first book award from Texas Tech University Press, which published her collection, *The Love That Ended Yesterday in Texas.* Her work has appeared in *Atlantic, Georgia Review, Southern Review,* and several other journals.

Christopher Buckley's eighth book of poetry, *Camino Cielo,* will be published by Orchises Press of Alexandria, Virginia, in January 1997. In 1994 the University of Nevada Press published his collection of creative nonfiction, *Cruising State: Growing up in Southern California* and with Christopher Merrill he edited the anthology *What Will*

Suffice: Contemporary American Poets on the Art of Poetry (Peregrine Smith Books, 1995).

W. E. Butts has published recently in *Calliope, Defined Providence*, and *Mid-American Review*. He is the author of several chapbooks and a full-length collection, *The Required Dance* (Igneus Press), which includes the poem "Martin's Nursing Home," anthologized here. He received an MFA in Writing from Vermont College, and he currently teaches in the Continuing Education Department at the University of New Hampshire.

Grace Cavalieri has published poetry, plays and short stories and teaches writing in colleges and workshops throughout the U.S. Among other honors, she holds the Allen Ginsberg Award for Poetry, the PEN Syndicated Fiction Award, and the Silver Medal from the Corporation for Public Broadcasting. She produces and hosts the longstanding program *The Poet and the Poem* on public radio.

David Chorlton has shown his art work, mostly watercolors, in exhibitions in Austria and the United States. He has published several chapbooks of poetry, one of which, *The Insomniacs*, won the 1994 Slipstream contest. He is active in peace, justice and environmental groups in the Phoenix area, and his opinion pieces and articles have appeared in the *Mesa Tribune, The Phoenix Gazette, Dry Heat*, and other publications.

Lyn Coffin's books of poems include *Human Trappings* and *The Poetry of Wickedness*. She has also translated books of poetry by Anna Akhmatova, Jaroslav Seifert, and Jiri Orten. She is

an Associate Editor of *Michigan Quarterly Review*.

Rhea L. Cohen is an environmental specialist for the Army Corps of Engineers. Her chapbooks have won first prize in two state competitions: *Message From Mid-River* (Avonelle Associates, Ltd., Columbus, Ohio, 1980), and *Time of Two Lights* (Montpelier Cultural Arts Center, Laurel, Maryland, 1989). Her poems have appeared in *New Yorker Magazine, Emrys Journal, Asheville Arts Journal* and other publications.

Geraldine Connolly is the author of two poetry collections, *The Red Room*, and *Food for the Winter*. She has been awarded two N.E.A. fellowships, a Maryland Arts Council fellowship and the Carolyn Kizer Award from Poetry Northwest. Her work has appeared recently in *Poetry, The Plum Review, Hampden-Sydney Poetry Review, The Gettysburg Review*, and *Chelsea*. She has co-edited *Poet Lore* since 1993.

Ann Darr has published eight collections of her poems and recently edited the 20th anniversary anthology for Washington Writers' Publishing House, *Hungry As We Are*, poems by Washington area poets. In April she was featured at the New York Museum of TV and Radio. A pilot for the Air Force during World War II, she has recently returned to flying. She is at work on a new collection of poems about traveling with the American Wind Symphony Orchestra in Europe. She teaches at American University and The Writer's Center in Bethesda, Maryland.

Michael C. Davis has been a dishwasher, gardener, abstractor, indexer, theater set builder, and newsletter

writer. At the moment, he is a copy
editor for the Bureau of National
Affairs. His poetry has appeared in *Poet
Lore* and *Lip Service*. In 1989, he was a
finalist in the Lip Service Poetry and
Prose series competition. He has read
at the Miller Cabin Series, the Writer's
Center, and the Library of Congress
Noontime Series, and at other venues
in the Washington, D.C. area.

Moshe Dor is the author of more than
30 books and the recipient of the Bialik
Prize, Israel's top literary honor. His
most recent book in English translation
is *Khamsin: Memoirs and Poetry by a
Native Israeli* (Three Continents Press,
1994).

Thomas Dorsett is the author of *Dance,
Fire, Dance* (Icarus Books, 1993). His
poems have appeared in *Confrontation,
Piedmont Literary Journal, Verse, Webster
Review, Wisconsin Review*, and several
other journals and anthologies.

Denise Duhamel is the author of four
full-length poetry books: *Kinky, Girl
Soldier, The Woman with Two Vaginas*, and
Smile!. She is also the author of four
chapbooks, the most recent of which is
How the Sky Fell.

Cornelius Eady is the author of five
volumes of poetry, including the 1985
Lamont Poetry Prize-winner *Victims of
the Latest Dance Craze*. His most recent
book, *you don't miss your water*, was
published by Henry Holt and Company
in 1995. He teaches at the State
University of New York at Stony Brook
and is Director of its Poetry Center.

Laura Fargas' first full-length collection
of poems, *An Animal of the Sixth Day*, was
published in 1996 by Texas Tech
University Press.

Jane Flanders is the author of three
poetry collections, most recently
Timepiece (University of Pittsburgh
Press). She lives in Pelham, New York,
and teaches in the Writing Institute at
Sarah Lawrence College.

Roland Flint has published six books
and three chapbooks of poems. His
collection, *Stubborn* (University of
Illinois Press, 1990), was selected by
Dave Smith for the National Poetry
Series.

Lillian Frankel is the author of 17
books in the juvenile How-to field. She
has written radio scripts and documen-
tary films for the U.S. Department of
Agriculture. Her poems have appeared
in *Calvert, Lip Service, Maryland Poetry
Review, San Miguel Writers*, and several
other publications, and her essays have
appeared in *The Washington Post*.

Nan Fry is an associate professor in the
Academic Studies Department at the
Corcoran School of Art and the author
of two books of poetry, *Relearning the
Dark* (Washington Writers' Publishing
House, 1991) and *Say What I Am Called*
(Sibyl-Child, 1988), a chapbook of
riddles she translated from the Anglo-
Saxon.

Brendan Galvin's tenth book, *Sky and
Island Light* was recently published by
Louisiana State University Press. Other
recent books include *Saints in Their Ox-
Hide Boat* (1992) and Wampanoag
Traveler (1989), both from LSU Press,
Great Blue: New and Selected Poems
(1990), published from the University
of Illinois Press, and *Early Returns*
(1992) from Carnegie Mellon. In 1991
Ampersand Press published *Outer Life:
The Poetry of Brendan Galvin* (Martha
Christina, editor), containing five essays
on his work, an interview, and a

complete bibliography of his poems. Galvin received the Charity Randall Citation of the International Poetry Forum in 1994, and the first O.B. Hardison Jr. Poetry Prize from the Folger Shakespeare Library in 1991.

Martin Galvin has published two books of poetry, including *Wild Card* (Washington Writers' Publishing House), which was selected by Howard Nemerov for the Washington Poetry Committee Prize for 1989. His poem "Hilda and Me and Hazel" won *Poet Lore*'s 1990 John Williams Andrews Narrative Poetry Prize. His poems have appeared recently in *Bogg, Poem, Poet and Critic, Four Quarters, The G.W. Review,* and *Poetry.* He has taught English at Walt Whitman High School and elsewhere for the last thirty years.

Margaret Gibson has published five books with LSU Press. *Long Walks in the Afternoon* was the Lamont Selection for 1982; *Memories of the Future* was co-winner of the Melville Cane Award in 1986-87; *The Vigil,* a finalist for the 1993 National Book Award. *Earth Elegy: New and Selected Poems* is forthcoming in 1997.

Albert Goldbarth has been publishing collections of poetry for over two decades. They include, among others, *Heaven and Earth,* recipient of the National Book Critics Circle Award, and *Adventures in Ancient Egypt* (Ohio State University Press). David R. Godine will publish *Beyond* in late 1997. Mr. Goldbarth lives in Wichita, Kansas.

Barbara Goldberg is the author of five books, most recently, *Marvelous Pursuits,* winner of the Violet Reed Haas Award (Snake Nation Press, 1995). The recipient of two fellowships from The National Endowment for the Arts, she

has been an editor of *Poet Lore* and is currently director of editorial services of the American Speech-Language-Hearing Association.

Erella Hadar has served as cultural attaché at the Israeli embassy in Washington, D.C.

Moishe Leib Halpern (1886-1932) has been called by Irving Howe "perhaps the most original poet in Yiddish." He was born in the Galician village of Zlochev, moved to Vienna at twelve, and became editor of the Montreal *People's Journal* in 1912. His books include *To New York* (1919) and *The Golden Peacock* (1924).

William Heyen is Professor of English and Poet in Residence at SUNY Brockport. The recipient of Fulbright, Guggenheim, NEA, and American Academy and Institute of Arts and Letters awards, he is the author of *Erika: Poems of the Holocaust, Ribbons: The Gulf War,* and *The Host: Selected Poems 1965-1990.* Most recently, his *Crazy Horse in Stillness,* a collection of 450 poems, has appeared from BOA Editions.

David Hilton has taught English at Anne Arundel Community College in Arnold, Maryland, since 1971. He is author of *Huladance* (Crossing Press) and *No Relation to the Hotel* (Coffee House Press). His poems have appeared in *Poetry, Poetry Northwest, Chicago Review, Iowa Review, Beloit Poetry Journal, Exquisite Corpse,* and several other journals.

Edward Haworth Hoeppner is the author of *Echoes and Moving Fields: Structure and Subjectivity in the Poetry of W. S. Merwin and John Ashbery.* He has published 100 poems in various journals and magazines, including *Boulevard, The Denver Quarterly, The Indiana Review, The Ohio Review, Poetry East,* and *Prairie Schooner.*

William Holland has published poetry and fiction in many magazines and has received several writing grants. Some of Us Press published a book of his poems in 1973. He is also a musician and recording artist with five albums to his credit.

Jean Janzen lives in Fresno, California, where she teaches poetry writing at Fresno Pacific College and in the public schools. She also teaches at Eastern Mennonite University in Virginia. A recipient of an NEA award in 1995, her most recent publication is *Snake in the Parsonage* (Good Books, 1995). Other collections are *The Upside-Down Tree* (Windflower, Winnepeg, 1992), and *Three Mennonite Poets* (Good Books, 1986).

Philip K. Jason has edited or co-edited *Poet Lore* since 1979. The most recent of his three collections is *The Separation* (Vietnam Generation, 1995). He has written or edited several books of criticism.

Rod Jellema, twice an NEA Fellow in poetry and founding director of the creative writing program at the University of Maryland, now leads workshops at the Writer's Center. His latest book is *The Eighth Day: New and Selected Poems* (Dryad Press). Recent poems of his have been in *Plum, Field,* and *WordWrights!*.

Shirley Kaufman's newest book is *Roots in the Air: New and Selected Poems*, published by Copper Canyon Press. She is the author of six other collections of poetry and translations of the Israeli

poets Abba Kovner and Amir Gilboa. She has lived in Jerusalem since 1973.

Deborah Kilgore has recent work in *Slate Run Review, Nerve Cowboy,* and *Agnieska's Dowry.* She is a poet and professional student in Austin and College Station, Texas.

Aaron Kramer's most recent collections of poems include *Indigo and Other Poems* (1991), *The Burning Bush* (1983) and *In Wicked Times* (1983). In 1989 his translations of 135 Yiddish poets were published in *A Century of Yiddish Poetry.* A selected edition of his poems, *Border Incident,* translated into Russian, was recently issued in St. Petersburg.

Dorianne Laux is author of two collections of poetry from BOA Editions, *Awake* (1990) and *What We Carry* (1994), which was a finalist for the National Book Critics Circle Award. She is also the recipient of a Pushcart Prize and a fellowship from The National Endowment for the Arts. In 1994 she joined the faculty at the University of Oregon's Program in Creative Writing. Her poems have appeared in *American Poetry Review, The Harvard Review, The Southern Review, The Alaska Quarterly Review,* and other journals.

Barbara F. Lefcowitz has published five poetry collections, most recently *The Minarets of Vienna* (1996). She has also published a novel and is now completing a mystery novel.

Merrill Leffler has published *Partly Pandemonium, Partly Love,* a collection of poems, and edited *The Changing Orders: Poetry from Israel* (*Poet Lore*). He is translating, with Moshe Dor, poems by the late Israeli poet Eytan Eytan that will be published as *A Guest in Your Own Body.*

Mitchell LesCarbeau is a winner of the Discovery/*The Nation* Prize, the Grolier Award, and he has been a fellow at Yaddo and Dorland Mountain Colony. He has published in *Three Penny Review, The Nation, Carolina Quarterly* and elsewhere, and he teaches at Green Mountain College in Vermont.

Susan Ludvigson's most recent collection of poems is *Trinity* (LSU Press, 1996). She teaches at Winthrop University in Rock Hill, South Carolina.

Kevin MacDonald was born in Washington, D.C., and has exhibited regularly since 1974. He studied at the Corcoran School of Art and Montgomery College, and received a BFA from George Washington University. His work is in the collections of the Corcoran Gallery of Art, the Phillips Collection, the Hirshhorn Museum, the National Museum of American Art, the Baltimore Museum of Art, and the Metropolitan Museum of Art, as well as numerous private and corporate collections. He is represented by the David Adamson Gallery.

David McAleavey teaches English at George Washington University. He is author of *Holding Obsidian*, (Washington Writers' Publishing House, 1985) and he recently wrote a poem commissioned by George Washington University to be set to choral music by Steve Hilmy as part of the University's 175th anniversary celebration.

Walter McDonald has published sixteen collections of poems and stories, including *Counting Survivors* (University of Pittsburgh Press, 1995). Other books include *After the Noise of Saigon* (University of Massachusetts Press), and *Night Landings* (HarperCollins). His poems have appeared in *American Poetry Review, The Atlantic, The Kenyon Review, Poetry, The Paris Review, Prairie Schooner, New England Review*, and several other journals.

Elaine Magarrell has published two books of poetry, *On Hogback Mountain* (Washington Writers' Publishing House) and *Blameless Lives* (The Word Works Washington Prize, 1991). She also writes short stories.

William Matthews' most recent books are *Time & Money* (Houghton Mifflin) and a collection of translations, *The Mortal City: 100 Epigrams of Martial* (Ohio Review Books), both published in 1995.

José Antonio Mazzotti is from Lima, Peru, and teaches Spanish at Temple University. The author of four books of poetry, his work has been widely anthologized in Mexico, Cuba, and now the United States. Most recently, he co-edited *El busque de los huesos*, a critical anthology of contemporary Peruvian poetry.

Peter Meinke has published five books in the University of Pittsburgh Poetry Series, most recently *Scars* and *Liquid Paper: New & Selected Poems*. His collection of short stories, *The Piano Tuner*, won the 1986 Flannery O'Connor Award. His poems have appeared in *The New Yorker, The New Republic, Poetry, The Georgia Review, Yankee, Grand Street*, and several other journals.

William Meredith's first book of poems, *Love Letter from an Impossible Land*, was selected by Archibald Macleish in 1944 for the Yale Series of Younger Poets. He has published several books of poems, including *Partial Accounts*, which won the Pulitzer Prize and the Los Angeles

Times Book Award in 1988. He is a Chancellor Emeritus of the Academy of American Poets, and he served as Poetry Consultant to the Library of Congress from 1978 to 1980.

Leonard Nathan has new poems forthcoming in *Poet Lore, The New Yorker*, and *Wilderness*. Graywolf Press recently published his *Diary of a Left-Handed Birdwatcher*.

Howard Nemerov served as America's Poet Laureate from 1988 to 1990. He received many awards, including the first Theodore Roethke Memorial Award, The Pulitzer Prize for Poetry, The National Book Award and the Bollingen Prize for Poetry. He published more than three dozen books of poetry, fiction and criticism, and he served as the Edward Mallinckrodt Distinguished University Professor of English at Washington University in St. Louis.

Jean Nordhaus has served as President of Washington Writers' Publishing House and Coordinator of Poetry Programs at the Folger Shakespeare Library. Her third book of poems, *My Life in Hiding*, appeared in *Quarterly Review of Literature*, Vol. XXX. She lives in Washington, D.C.

Sharon Olds was born in San Francisco, in 1942, and attended Stanford University (B.A., 1964) and Columbia University (Ph.D., 1972). *The Wellspring*, her fifth collection, was published by Knopf in January 1996. Her other books are *The Father* (shortlisted for the T.S. Eliot Award in England), *The Gold Cell, Satan Says*, and *The Dead and the Living*, which was chosen as the Lamont Poetry Selection by The Academy of American Poets and received the National Book Critics Circle Award. Ms. Olds teaches

in the Graduate Creative Writing Program at New York University, and for twelve years has helped run a writing workshop at the Sigismund Goldwater Memorial Hospital, a 900-bed public hospital for the severely physically disabled.

Eric Pankey is the author of *For The New Year, Heartwood, Apocrypha*, and *The Late Romances*. He teaches at George Mason University.

Linda Pastan has received fellowships from the National Endowment for the Arts and from the Maryland State Arts Council. She has won the Dylan Thomas Award, the Di Castagnola Award, the Bess Hokin Prize of *Poetry* magazine, and several other awards. Her ninth book of poems, *An Early Afterlife*, was recently issued in paperback by Norton.

Walter Pavlich's latest book, *Running near the End of the World*, is available from the University of Iowa Press. His work has appeared in *The Atlantic Monthly, The Yale Review, Poetry, American Poetry Review*, and many other journals. He lives in Northern California, and his email address is wpavlich@aol.com.

Richard Peabody was born and raised in the Washington, D.C. area. He edited *Gargoyle* magazine from 1976 to 1990. He is co-editor of the *Mondo Barbie, Mondo Elvis, Mondo Marilyn*, and *Mondo James Dean* anthologies, and he teaches fiction writing at Johns Hopkins University and the Writer's Center in Bethesda, Maryland. His most recent book of poems is *Buoyance and Other Myths* (Gut Punch Press, 1995).

Robert Peters has published forty volumes of poetry, a dozen collections of essays and critical studies, and has writen one-man plays on such figures as Mad Ludwig of Bavaria, the Hungarian Blood Countess Elizabeth Bathory, and the Shaker mystic Ann Lee. His most recent books include *Poems Selected and New* (Asylum Arts), *Where the Bee Sucks: Workers, Drones, and Queens of Contemporary Poetry* (Asylum), and a series of memoirs from the University of Wisconsin Press, including *Crunching Gravel: On Growing Up in the Thirties* and *Nell's Story: A Woman from Eagle River.*

Mary Quattlebaum is the author of seven award-winning children's books and director of Arts Project Renaissance, a creative writing program for older adults. Her poetry has been published in *Gettysburg Review, Antietam Review,* and other literary journals.

John Robert Quinn has had work published in *Poetry, The New Yorker, New York Times, America, Commonweal, The Christian Science Monitor,* and several other publications.

G. J. Racz's translation of Benito Pérez Galdós' historical novel *Gerona* was published by the Edwin Mellen Press. His translations of the Andalusian poet José Manuel del Pino and the Peruvian José Antonio Mazzotti have appeared in several journals. Most recently, a selection of his translations of the experimental Argentine *Xul* poets was put out by Roof Books.

Marilee Richards works for an adoption agency. She has received a grant from the California Arts Council. Her work has been published in *Poetry Northwest, Southern Review, Cimarron Review, Southern Poetry Review,* and other journals.

Trish Rucker is a freelance writer in Atlanta. She has been the recipient of

two Georgia Council for the Arts grants. Her stories and poems have appeared in more than 30 literary journals, including *New Orleans Review, The Sun: A Magazine of Ideas,* and *The Centennial Review.* Her first novel, *Dancing With Gabriel,* is currently being considered for publication.

Benjamin Saltman has published seven books of poems, the most recent of which is *The Sun Takes Us Away: New and Selected Poems* (Red Hen Press, 1996). He has received several awards and fellowships including two NEA awards and a Chester A. Jones Foundation Award. He is Emeritus Professor of English at California State University, Northridge.

Catherine Harnett Shaw is the author of *Still Life* and has published poetry in such journals as *American Literary Review, Yankee, The Chatahoochee Review, Fine Madness, Gargoyle,* and *Negative Capability.* She works in the criminal justice system and has another manuscript, *Evidence,* which she is looking to publish.

Enid Shomer's poems and stories have appeared in *The New Yorker, The Atlantic, Poetry,* and other journals. Her recent books include *This Close to the Earth* (University of Arkansas Press) and *Imaginary Men,* winner of the Iowa Fiction Prize. A new book of poems, *Black Drum,* is forthcoming in 1997. Shomer has received two grants from the NEA, and three from the State of Florida, all in poetry.

Layle Silbert, whose poems appear in several journals and anthologies, has published a book of poems, *Making a Baby in Union Park Chicago* (Downtown Poets). He is also the author of *Imaginary People & Other Strangers* (Exile

Press), *Gurkah & Other Stories* (Host Publications), and *New York New York* (St. Andrews—forthcoming).

Myra Sklarew, whose most recent collection is *Lithuania: New & Selected Poems* (1995, Azul Editions), is starting a project with the working title *Holocaust and the Construction of Memory.*

R. T. Smith's books include *The Cardinal Heart* (Livingston Press, 1991) and *Trespasses* (LSU, 1996). He has received fellowships from the NEA and Arts International, and he is editor of *Shenandoah*, at Washington and Lee University.

Andrew Sofer's poems have appeared in *The Formalist, Folio,* and *Phoebe.* He was a 1994 finalist in the Howard Nemerov Sonnet Award Competition, and he is completing a Ph.D. in English at the University of Michigan, Ann Arbor.

Katherine Soniat's collection, *A Shared Life,* won the Iowa Poetry Prize from the University of Iowa Press (1993). Her work is in recent issues of *Threepenny Review, River Styx, American Voice* and *Manoa: A Journal of the Pacific Rim.*

Stephanie Strickland's third full-length collection, *True North,* will be published in 1996 as the Sandeen Poetry Prize by the University of Notre Dame Press. *True North* was also the 1995 winner of the Poetry Society of America's Di Castagnola Prize for a work in progress. Strickland's second collection, *The Red Virgin: A Poem of Simone Weil,* was awarded the 1993 University of Wisconsin Press Brittingham Prize, and her first volume of poems, *Give the Body Back,* was published in 1991 by the University of Missouri Press.

Sue Teigen has published poetry in the *Sonora Review, Northwest Review, Indiana Review* and elsewhere. She lives and works in Montgomery County, Maryland.

Hilary Tham is the author of five books of poetry, most recently *Men & Other Strange Myths.* Her book of memoirs *Lane with no name* is forthcoming from Three Continents Press in 1996. Her work has appeared in *International Quarterly, Kerem, Poets On,* and other journals. She teaches writing in the schools and is a poetry editor for *The Potomac Review* and *The Word Works* Press.

Naomi Thiers has lived in Washington, D.C. since 1980. In 1992, her collection of poems, *Only the Raw Hands Are Heaven,* was published by Washington Writers' Publishing House. Her poetry, fiction and journalism have been published in many magazines, and she teaches writing at American University.

Lee Upton's third book of poems, *Approximate Darling,* was published by the University of Georgia Press in 1996. Bucknell University Press also recently published her second book of criticism, *Obsession and Release: Rereading the Poetry of Louise Bogan.* Her poems and fiction appear widely.

Lloyd Van Brunt has just completed a memoir-novel, *I Fall in Love with Nancy Drew,* and is presently at work on a novel, *Pretty People.*

William Van Wert teaches film and creative writing at Temple University. He won last year's national AWP competition in creative nonfiction, the result of which is a book of essays, *Memory Links,* published by University of Georgia Press. He has three novels forthcoming: *Don Quickshot* (Swallow's Tale Press), *When Arm & Hammer Met the Pillsbury Doughboy* (Simon & Schuster) and *Stool Wives* (Plover Press). He also has a forthcoming book of poems, *Proper Myth* (Orchises Press). "Playing With Fire" is one of several longer poems that are part of a collection called "Move Through the Body."

David Walker's four published books of poems include *Moving Out* (1976), which was winner of the Associated Writing Programs Poetry Award (University Press of Virginia), and *Voiceprints* (Romulus Editions), which received a publication grant from the NEA. His poems also appear in *The Maine Reader*, an anthology published by Houghton Mifflin in 1991.

Ronald Wallace's nine books include *Time's Fancy* and *The Makings of Happiness*, both from the University of Pittsburgh Press. He directs the creative writing program at Wisconsin and edits the University of Wisconsin Press poetry series.

T. H. S. Wallace's books of poetry include *Beyond the Neat Houses Cheap Talk Built* (Linwood Press, 1988) and *Raw on the Bars of Longing* (Rabbit Press, 1994). His work has appeared in *Mid-American Review, Swanee Review, Sonoma Mandala, Southern Poetry Review, Cumberland Review,* and other journals.

Nancy G. Westerfield won the Benét Narrative Poem Award in 1991. She has since been an NEA Fellow, and a guest twice at Yaddo. Her first appearance in *Poet Lore*, in 1968, was shared with her husband Hargis: a group of their railroad pieces which J. W. Andrews titled "High Iron."

Theodore Worozbyt has had recent acceptances from *Prairie Schooner, Northwest Review, Tar River Poetry, Kenyon Review,* and *Poetry.* He has received grants from the NEA and the Georgia Council for the Arts, and his first book manuscript, *The Lone Eye*, is in search of a publisher.

Paul Zimmer has published eleven books of poetry, including *Family Reunion* (University of Pittsburgh Press, 1985), which won an Award for Literature from the American Academy and Institute of Arts and Letters, *The Great Bird of Love* (University of Illinois Press, 1989), which was selected by William Stafford for the National Poetry Series, *Big Blue Train* (University of Arkansas Press, 1993), and *Crossing to Sunlight: Selected Poems* (University of Georgia Press, 1996). He has served as Associate Director of the University of Pittsburgh Press and Director of the University of Georgia Press, and he is currently director of the University of Iowa Press.

Linda Zisquit is a graduate of Tufts University, Harvard University, and the Writing Program at the State University of New York at Buffalo. She lives in Jerusalem, Israel, where she translates and teaches. Her poems have appeared in *The Literary Review, Ploughshares, Stand* (UK), *Three Rivers Poetry Journal*, and other journals. A book of her poems, *Ritual Bath*, was published by Broken Moon Press in 1993.

Acknowledgments

All poems © by the authors and/or translators in the year indicated below.

Henry Allen. "Japanese Ambassador" *Poet Lore* Vol. 79 No. 4 © 1985

Paul Allen. "Youngblood Tells Beekman and Jimmy Jr. About Crow" *Poet Lore* Vol. 82, No. 1 © 1987

Yehuda Amichai. (trans. Chana Bloch). From "Songs of Zion the Beautiful" *Poet Lore* Vol. 81, No. 2 © 1986

Susan Astor. "The Wife of God" *Poet Lore* Vol. 76, No. 2. "Neighbors" *Poet Lore* Vol. 77, No. 2 © 1982

Mark H. Baechtel. "Window, North Charles Street" first published in *Poet Lore* Vol. 80, No. 3 as "Staying" © 1985

John Balaban. "For My Sister in Warminster General Hospital" *Poet Lore* Vol. 83, No. 3 © 1988. "Snowbound" *Poet Lore* Vol. 81, No. 3 © 1986. Both collected in *Words for My Daughter* © 1991 by John Balaban. Reprinted by permission of Copper Canyon Press, PO Box 271, Port Townsend, WA 98368.

Michelle Boisseau. "Timbre" *Poet Lore* Vol. 85, No. 3 © 1990

Cathy Smith Bowers. "Conversation with My Hyphen After the Divorce" *Poet Lore* Vol. 81, No. 4 © 1987. "Thunder" *Poet Lore* Vol. 84, No. 3 © 1989. "Thunder" reprinted with permission from *Love That Ended Yesterday in Texas*, © 1992, Texas Tech University Press.

Christopher Buckley. "Prima Facie" *Poet Lore* Vol. 87, No. 2 © 1992

W. E. Butts. "Martin's Nursing Home" *Poet Lore* Vol. 84, No. 1 © 1989

Grace Cavalieri. "Les Jardins" *Poet Lore* Vol. 77, No. 2 © 1982

David Chorlton. "St. John of the Cross in the Carmelite Priory, Toledo, 1578" *Poet Lore* Vol. 78, No. 2 © 1983

Lyn Coffin. "Stone Wine" *Poet Lore* Vol. 76, No. 2 © 1981

Rhea L. Cohen. "Mary Cassatt, Pupil of Edgar Degas" *Poet Lore* Vol. 77, No. 4 © 1983

Geraldine Connolly. "Climbing Up to the Attic" *Poet Lore* Vol. 80, No. 1 © 1985

Ann Darr. "What Do You Want from the Country?" *Poet Lore* Vol. 80, No. 3 © 1985

Michael C. Davis. "Hrasno" *Poet Lore* Vol. 90, No. 4 © 1996

Moshe Dor. "Basic Vocabulary" (trans. Shaw), *Poet Lore* Vol. 85, No. 4 © 1991. "Responsibility" (trans. Moshe Dor, Erella Hadar, and Myra Sklarew), *Poet Lore* Vol. 81, No. 2 © 1986

Thomas Dorsett. "The Arsonist" *Poet Lore* Vol. 77, No. 3 © 1982

Denise Duhamel. "Literary Barbie" *Poet Lore* Vol. 87, No. 4 © 1993

Cornelius Eady. "Miss Johnson Dances for the First Time" *Poet Lore* Vol. 79, No. 1 © 1984

Laura Fargas. "Psyche" *Poet Lore* Vol. 87, No. 1 © 1992. Reprinted with permission from *An Animal of the Sixth Day*, by Laura Fargas, copyright 1996 Texas Tech University Press, 1-800-832-4042.

Jane Flanders. "John Keats, Apothecary" *Poet Lore* Vol. 80, No. 2 © 1985

Roland Flint. "Pigeon in the Night" *Poet Lore* Vol. 76, No. 2 © 1981

Lillian Frankel. "Ten Years After She Dies My Mother Teaches Me How to Sew" *Poet Lore* Vol. 83, No. 2 © 1988

Nan Fry. "Night-Tide" *Poet Lore* Vol. 75, No. 4 © 1981

Brendan Galvin. "Hitting the Wall" *Poet Lore* Vol. 77, No. 3 © 1982

Martin Galvin. "Country Play" *Poet Lore* Vol. 75, No. 3 © 1981. "Learning the Trade" Poet Lore Vol. 81, No. 4 © 1987

Margaret Gibson. "Catechism Elegy" *Poet Lore* Vol. 76, No. 1 © 1981. From *Long Walks in the Afternoon* (LSU Press), by Margaret Gibson. Copyright © by Margaret Gibson. Used with permission.

Albert Goldbarth. "Images of the Soul" *Poet Lore* Vol. 78, No. 1 © 1983. "The Ways" *Poet Lore* Vol. 79, No. 1 © 1984

Barbara Goldberg. "When I Learn My Friend Must Lose Her Breast to Cancer" *Poet Lore* Vol. 83, No. 1 © 1988

Moishe Leib Halpern. (trans. Aaron Kramer). "Bread and Fire" *Poet Lore* Vol. 76, No. 2 © 1981

William Heyen. "Stiletto" *Poet Lore* Vol. 84, No. 1 © 1989

David Hilton. "The Old Hog Farm" *Poet Lore* Vol. 89, No. 2 © 1994

Edward Haworth Hoeppner. "War Correspondence" *Poet Lore* Vol. 91, No. 1 © 1996

William Holland. "Notebook" *Poet Lore* Vol. 77, No. 4 © 1983

Jean Janzen. "Every Year the Bodies" *Poet Lore* Vol. 78, No. 2 © 1983

Rod Jellema. "Trout Run" *Poet Lore* Vol. 77, No. 3 © 1982

□ *Acknowledgments* □

Shirley Kaufman. "Drifting" *Poet Lore* Vol. 81, No. 2 © 1986. Collected in *Roots in the Air* © 1996 by Shirley Kaufman. Reprinted by permission of Copper Canyon Press, PO Box 271, Port Townsend, WA 98368.

Deborah Kilgore. "Strange Temptation" *Poet Lore* Vol. 90, No. 4 © 1996

Dorianne Laux. "Quarter to Six" *Poet Lore* Vol. 80, No. 2 © 1985

Barbara F. Lefcowitz. "Sarabande" *Poet Lore* Vol. 90, No. 3 © 1995

Merrill Leffler. "Metaphor" *Poet Lore* Vol. 87, No. 1 © 1992

Mitchell LesCarbeau. "The Persistence of Polytheism" *Poet Lore* Vol. 89, No. 2 © 1994

Susan Ludvigson. from the series "Letters Back: God Writes to Emily Dickinson" *Poet Lore* Vol. 91, No. 1 © 1996

Elaine Magarrell. "Deciduous" *Poet Lore* Vol. 85, No. 1 © 1990

William Matthews. "A Small Greasefire in the Kitchen" *Poet Lore* Vol. 91, No. 2 © 1996

José Antonio Mazzotti (trans. Gregary J. Racz). "Mare is the Female of the Horse" *Poet Lore* Vol. 89, No. 1 © 1994

David McAleavey. "Construction (II)" *Poet Lore* Vol. 85, No. 2 © 1990

Walter McDonald. "After Eden" *Poet Lore* Vol. 80, No. 4 © 1986

Peter Meinke. "Grandfather at the Pool" *Poet Lore* Vol. 76, No. 4 © 1982

William Meredith. "Rurals" *Poet Lore* Vol. 75, No. 2 © 1980

Leonard Nathan. "Them" *Poet Lore* Vol. 79, No. 1 © 1984

Howard Nemerov. "Waste" *Poet Lore* Vol. 85, No. 3 © 1990

Jean Nordhaus. "Wood" *Poet Lore* Vol. 76, No. 2 © 1981

Sharon Olds. "The Morning After Kristallnacht" *Poet Lore* Vol. 83, No. 1 © 1988. "The Creature" (first published as "The Beast" in *Poet Lore* Vol. 83, No. 1) © 1988

Eric Pankey. "The Gift" *Poet Lore* Vol. 77, No. 1 © 1982

Linda Pastan. "By the Mailbox" *Poet Lore* Vol. 75, No. 1 © 1980. "Song" *Poet Lore* Vol. 75, No. 3 © 1980. Both poems published in *Waiting for My Life* (W.W. Norton, 1981).

Walter Pavlich. "Pistachios" *Poet Lore* Vol. 88, No. 2 © 1993

Richard Peabody. "She Discovers Jazz" *Poet Lore* Vol. 86, No. 3 © 1991

Robert Peters. "Cape Misery" *Poet Lore* Vol. 80, No. 3 © 1985

Mary Quattlebaum. "The Statue Speaks with Pygmalion" *Poet Lore* Vol. 85, No. 4 © 1991

John Robert Quinn. "The Dream" *Poet Lore* Vol. 84, No. 3 © 1989

Marilee Richards. "How an Older Man Makes Love" *Poet Lore* Vol. 89, No. 4 © 1995

Trish Rucker. "Fate, Like Jayne Mansfield, Takes a Road Trip" *Poet Lore* Vol. 86, No. 3 © 1991

Benjamin Saltman. "Cloudy and Isaac" *Poet Lore* Vol. 84, No. 1 © 1989

Catherine Harnett Shaw. "Child Bride" *Poet Lore* Vol. 85, No. 3 © 1990

Enid Shomer. "Luncheonette, Live Oak, Florida" *Poet Lore* Vol. 79, No. 4 © 1985

Layle Silbert. "My True Hand" *Poet Lore* Vol. 76, No. 4 © 1982

Myra Sklarew. "Exchange" *Poet Lore* Vol. 75, No. 4 © 1981

R.T. Smith. "No Masks" *Poet Lore* Vol. 77, No. 2 © 1982

Andrew Sofer. "The Anatomy of Whales" *Poet Lore* Vol. 88, No. 2 © 1993

Katherine Soniat. "War" *Poet Lore* Vol. 83, No. 3 © 1988. Reprinted with permission from *A Shared Life* (University of Iowa Press, 1993).

Stephanie Strickland. "American Speech" *Poet Lore* Vol. 90, No. 3 © 1995. From *True North* by Stephanie Strickland. © 1996 by the University of Notre Dame Press. Reprinted by permission.

Sue Teigen. "Inside the Wolf" *Poet Lore* Vol. 84, No. 2 © 1989

Hilary Tham. "Letter from Malaysia" *Poet Lore* Vol. 79, No. 3 © 1984

Naomi Thiers. "Good News" *Poet Lore* Vol. 86, No. 4 © 1992

Lee Upton. "Mud Dog" *Poet Lore* Vol. 79, No. 2 © 1984

Lloyd Van Brunt. "Sidestep" *Poet Lore* Vol. 75, No. 2 © 1980

William Van Wert. "Playing with Fire" *Poet Lore* Vol. 90, No. 1 © 1995

David Walker. "Teaching the Dark" *Poet Lore* Vol. 76, No. 2 © 1981

Ronald Wallace. "At the Vietnamese Restaurant" *Poet Lore* Vol. 90, No. 1 © 1995

T. H. S. Wallace. "Imperatives" *Poet Lore* Vol. 79, No. 3 © 1984

Nancy G. Westerfield. "On Railroad Street" *Poet Lore* Vol. 84, No. 1 © 1989

Theodore Worozbyt. "Napoleon's Snuffbox" *Poet Lore* Vol. 88, No. 4 © 1994

Paul Zimmer. "Fritz, the Adjuster" *Poet Lore* Vol. 75, No. 1 © 1980

Linda Zisquit. "Song of Myself." *Poet Lore* Vol. 81, No. 2 © 1986

Ludvigson □ David McAleavey □ Walter McDonald □ Elaine Magarrell □ William Matthews □ José Antonio Mazzotti □ Peter Meinke □ William Meredith □ Leonard Nathan □ Howard Nemerov □ Jean Nordhaus □ Sharon Olds □ Eric Pankey □ Linda Pastan □ Walter Pavlich □ Richard Peabody □ Robert Peters □ Mary Quattlebaum □ John Robert Quinn □ Marilee Richards □ Trish Rucker □ Benjamin Saltman □ Catherine Harnett Shaw □ Enid Shomer □ Layle Silbert □ Myra Sklarew □ R. T. Smith □ Andrew Sofer □ Katherine Soniat □ Stephanie Strickland □ Sue Teigen □ Hilary Tham □ Naomi Thiers □ Lee Upton □ Lloyd Van Brunt □ William Van Wert □ David Walker □ Ronald Wallace □ T. H. S. Wallace □ Nancy G. Westerfield □ Theodore Worozbyt □ Paul Zimmer □ Linda Zisquit □ Henry Allen □ Paul Allen □ Yehuda Amichai □ Susan Astor □ Mark H. Baechtel □ John Balaban □ Michelle Boisseau □ Cathy Smith Bowers □ Christopher Buckley □ W. E. Butts □ Grace Cavalieri □ David Chorlton □ Lyn Coffin □ Rhea L. Cohen □ Geraldine Connolly □ Ann Darr □ Michael C. Davis □ Moshe Dor □ Thomas Dorsett □ Denise Duhamel □ Cornelius Eady □ Laura Fargas □ Jane Flanders □ Roland Flint □ Lillian Frankel □ Nan Fry □ Brendan Galvin □ Martin Galvin □ Margaret Gibson □ Albert Goldbarth □ Barbara Goldberg □ Moishe Leib Halpern □ William Heyen □ David Hilton □ Edward Haworth Hoeppner □ William Holland □ Jean Janzen □ Rod Jellema □ Shirley Kaufman □ Deborah Kilgore □ Dorianne Laux □ Barbara F. Lefcowitz □ Merrill Leffler □ Mitchell LesCarbeau □ Susan Ludvigson □ David McAleavey □ Walter McDonald □ Elaine Magarrell □ William Matthews □ José Antonio Mazzotti □ Peter Meinke □ William Meredith □ Leonard Nathan □ Howard Nemerov □ Jean Nordhaus □ Sharon Olds □ Eric Pankey □ Linda Pastan □ Walter Pavlich □ Richard Peabody □ Robert Peters □ Mary Quattlebaum □ John Robert Quinn □ Marilee Richards □ Trish Rucker □ Benjamin Saltman □ Catherine Harnett Shaw □ Enid Shomer □ Layle Silbert □ Myra Sklarew □ R. T. Smith □ Andrew Sofer □ Katherine Soniat □ Stephanie Strickland □ Sue Teigen □ Hilary Tham □ Naomi Thiers □ Lee Upton □ Lloyd Van Brunt □ William Van Wert □ David Walker □ Ronald Wallace □ T. H. S. Wallace □ Nancy G. Westerfield □ Theodore Worozbyt □ Paul Zimmer □ Linda Zisquit □ Henry Allen □ Paul Allen □